NEW
8.95

NEW ACCENTS
General Editor: TERENCE HAWKES

Reception Theory
A critical introduction

IN THE SAME SERIES:

* This title is not available from Methuen, Inc. in the USA

Reception Theory

A critical introduction

ROBERT C. HOLUB

METHUEN
London and New York

For my Mother

First published in 1984 by
Methuen, Inc.
733 Third Avenue, New York, NY 10017
Published in Great Britain by
Methuen & Co. Ltd
11 New Fetter Lane, London EC4P 4EE

© 1984 Robert C. Holub

Printed in the United States of America

Library of Congress Cataloging in Publication Data

Holub, Robert C.
Reception theory.
(New accents)
Bibliography: p.
Includes index.
1. Criticism – Germany (West) – History.
2. Reader-response criticism
– Germany (West)   3. Literature –
History and criticism.
I. Title   II. Series: New Accents (Methuen & Co.)
PT80.H64   1984   801'.95'0943   83-13385

ISBN 0-416-33580-2
ISBN 0-416-33590-X (pbk.)

British Library Cataloguing in Publication Data

Holub, Robert C.
Reception theory. – (New accents)
1. Criticism – Germany
I. Title   II. Series
801'.95'0943   PN99.G4

ISBN 0-416-33580-2
ISBN 0-416-33590-X Pbk

Contents

General editor's preface

It is easy to see that we are living in a time of rapid and radical social change. It is much less easy to grasp the fact that such change will inevitably affect the nature of those disciplines that both reflect our society and help to shape it.

Yet this is nowhere more apparent than in the central field of what may, in general terms, be called literary studies. Here, among large numbers of students at all levels of education, the erosion of the assumptions and presuppositions that support the literary disciplines in their conventional form has proved fundamental. Modes and categories inherited from the past no longer seem to fit the reality experienced by a new generation.

New Accents is intended as a positive response to the initiative offered by such a situation. Each volume in the series will seek to encourage rather than resist the process of change. To stretch rather than reinforce the boundaries that currently define literature and its academic study.

Some important areas of interest immediately present themselves. In various part of the world, new methods of analysis have been developed whose conclusions reveal the limitations of the Anglo-American outlook we inherit. New concepts of literary forms and modes have been proposed: new notions of the nature of literature itself, and of how it communicates, are current: new views of literature's role in relation to society flourish. *New Accents* will aim to expound and comment upon the most notable of these.

In the broad field of the study of human communication, more and more emphasis has been placed upon the nature and function of the new electronic media. *New Accents* will try to identify and discuss the challenge these offer to our traditional modes of critical response.

The same interest in communication suggests that the series should also concern itself with those wider anthropological and sociological areas of investigation which have begun to involve scrutiny of the nature of art itself and of its relation to our whole way of life. And this will ultimately require attention to be focused on some of those activities which in our society have hitherto been excluded from the prestigious realms of Culture. The disturbing realignment of values involved and the disconcerting nature of the pressures that work to bring it about both constitute areas that *New Accents* will seek to explore.

Finally, as its title suggests, one aspect of *New Accents* will be firmly located in contemporary approaches to language, and a continuing concern of the series will be to examine the extent to which relevant branches of linguistic studies can illuminate specific literary areas. The volumes with this particular interest will nevertheless presume no prior technical knowledge on the part of their readers, and will aim to rehearse the linguistics appropriate to the matter in hand, rather than to embark on general theoretical matters.

Each volume in the series will attempt an objective exposition of significant developments in its field up to the present as well as an account of its author's own views of the matter. Each will culminate in an informative bibliography as a guide to further study. And while each will be primarily concerned with matters relevant to its own specific interests, we can hope that a kind of conversation will be heard to develop between them; one whose accents may perhaps suggest the distinctive discourse of the future.

TERENCE HAWKES

Acknowledgements

Portions of my discussion of Iser appeared originally in an essay entitled "The American reception of reception theory," in *The German Quarterly*, vol. 55, no. 1, 1982, pp. 80–96. The section on Russian Formalism in chapter 2 was published in a slightly altered form under the title "Reception theory and Russian Formalism," in *Germano-Slavica*, vol. 3, no. 4, 1980, pp. 272–86. I am grateful to the editors of both journals for permission to use the material here. Thanks also go to the following for their kind permission to reproduce copyright material: Günter Waldmann and Wilhelm Fink GmbH & Co. for Figure 1 on p. 120; Norbert Groeben for Figure 2 on p. 138; and Hans Robert Jauss and the University of Minnesota Press for Table 1 on p. 80.

At various times during my work Christian Flemmer and Rick McCormick served as research assistants; Eric Mills and Viki Scott did the bulk of the typing. To them go my sincere thanks and appreciation. For their time and suggestions I am also indebted to those who read parts of the manuscript: Marc Blanchard, Christian Flemmer, Igor Hajek, Gerd Hillen, Robert Hughes, Simon Karlinsky, Richard Murphy, Hinrich Seeba, and John H. Smith. Special thanks go to Terence Hawkes for his careful reading of the manuscript and his many helpful suggestions; it is hard to imagine a more tolerant and encouraging general editor.

Preface

"Reception theory" is a term that is likely to sound strange to speakers of English who have not encountered it previously. As Hans Robert Jauss, one of the major proponents of this theory, noted humorously in 1979, to the foreign ear questions of "reception" may seem more appropriate to hotel management than to literature.[1] For followers of the German critical scene, however, the word "reception," alone or in one of its many compound forms, has been the key to theoretical concerns for the past decade and a half. No area of literary endeavor has been untouched by reception theory; indeed, traces of this method have affected adjacent disciplines like sociology and art history as well.

The proliferation of theoretical and practical investigations, though, has not produced conceptual unanimity, and what precisely reception studies entail is at present still a matter of dispute. Perhaps the central difficulty is determining exactly what the term means. One of the most persistent dilemmas, in fact, has been how *Rezeption* (reception) differs from *Wirkung* (usually rendered by "response" or "effect"). Both have to do with the impact of the work on someone, and it is not clear that they can be separated completely. None the less, the most frequent suggestion has been to view *Rezeption* as related to the reader, while *Wirkung* is supposed to pertain to textual aspects – an arrangement that is not entirely satisfactory by any account.

The difficulties are only multiplied, of course, by the facility with which compounds are formed in German. *Wirkungsgeschichte* (in the older sense of the "history of the impact" of a text or writer) has a long tradition of scholarship behind it in Germany, involving the examination of an author's influence on later generations, especially subsequent writers. How this study would differ from a *Rezeptionsgeschichte* (history of reception) or how a *Wirkungsästhetik* (aesthetics of effect or response) should be distinguished from a *Rezeptionsästhetik* (aesthetics of reception) are problems that have frequently surfaced over the course of the past two decades. These distinctions and the endeavors to refine terminology are not unimportant, of course. But in order to circumvent and simplify some of the possible confusion I have adopted the following policy: "reception theory" refers throughout to a general shift in concern from the author and the work to the text and the reader. It is used, therefore, as an umbrella term and encompasses both Jauss's and Iser's projects as well as empirical research and the traditional occupation with influences. The "aesthetics of reception," in contrast, is used only in connection with Jauss's early theoretical work. All other variations and compound uses should be easily understood in their context.

The reader acquainted with recent trends in American criticism will be more likely to wonder how reception theory relates to what has become known as "reader-response criticism" and why I have chosen to separate the Germans from other theorists dealing with apparently similar issues. The answers to these questions are related. Reader-response criticism, like reception theory, is an umbrella term that accommodates systems as diverse as Norman Holland's "transactive criticism," Jonathan Culler's structuralist poetics, and Stanley Fish's affective stylistics. It, too, refers to a general shift in attention from the author of the work to the text–reader pole, and, in fact, Wolfgang Iser, who will be discussed as one of the most important initiators of reception theory, is usually regarded as a "reader-response critic" as well.

What separates reader-response criticism from reception theory, however, are several important features. First and foremost, the designation itself is not the banner under which any of these critics campaigned; it has been applied *ex post facto* to a number of writers who have had very little contact with or influence on one another. These theorists are not participating in any critical movement, and they are apparently responding with their methods to quite different predecessors and circumstances. Reader-response critics are spread across the world, teaching at various institutions; they do not meet on any regular basis, nor do they publish in the same journals or attend the same conferences. The two most recent collections of writings by critics who have been gathered under this rubric provide ample evidence of the disparity of their various positions.[2] If reader-response criticism has become a critical force, as some would maintain, it is by virtue of the ingenuity of labeling rather than any commonality of effort.

Reception theory, by contrast, must be understood as a more cohesive, conscious, and collective undertaking. In the largest sense it is a reaction to social, intellectual, and literary developments in West Germany during the late 1960s. As we shall see in the first chapter, it emerged as a group effort on both the institutional and critical levels, involving a productive exchange of ideas among its advocates. Moreover, many adherents to this critical movement are associated with the University of Constance, either as professors, graduates, or participants in the biannual colloquia held there. The proceedings of these meetings, published under the series title *Poetik und Hermeneutik* (Poetics and Hermeneutics),[3] document the development and cohesiveness of this enterprise. Although not everyone who attends these conferences could be considered a reception theorist, the core group at least contains many of the scholars who have contributed most to the reorientation of West German literary theory that has gone under that name.

Finally, reception theory may be separated from reader-response criticism on the basis of lack of mutual influence. Aside from Iser, whose writings have received extensive coverage in both camps, there has been practically no contact between the two groups. Indeed, if footnotes are any indication of impact, the exchange between them has been non-existent. For all these reasons it seemed to me that a concentration on the West German theorists would allow for a more coherent – and, for readers of English, less familiar – account. The similarities in general critical perspective between reader-response criticism and reception theory are ultimately too superficial and too abstract for a merging here.

The main purpose of the following study is to introduce reception theory to those who have little or no knowledge of German. To this end I have included in the first two chapters material of an introductory nature. The first deals with a programmatic essay by Jauss on the development of literary scholarship and endeavors both to describe the intellectual and political climate in which reception theory emerged and to explain some of the reasons for its rapid acceptance. The second chapter examines some of the most important domestic and foreign influences on reception theory, the "precursors" to the development of a reader-oriented perspective in Germany. In the third and fourth chapters, on the other hand, the reception theorists themselves are the topic, while the closing remarks in the final chapter point to unresolved problems in reception theory in the context of modern criticism. To facilitate access for readers of English I have translated all quotations and titles from the German when no adequate English version could be found.

Although my target audience is one that is unfamiliar with the German critical scene, I trust that what I have written will have some interest for critics better acquainted with recent trends in German scholarship. While a good portion of what follows may not relate anything radically new for Germanists, I hope that it will provide either – at worst – a thorough and accurate review, or – at best – a stimulus for rethinking this important body of criticism. Finally, if the present volume plays any part in remedying the situation mentioned above by introducing reception theorists to reader-response critics, then it will have performed a useful function.

The change in paradigm and its socio-historical function

Paradigms in the history of criticism

In an essay of 1969 entitled "The change in the paradigm of literary scholarship,"[1] Hans Robert Jauss sketched the history of literary methods and postulated that the beginnings of a "revolution" in contemporary literary studies were at hand. Borrowing the concepts of "paradigm" and "scientific revolution" from the work of Thomas S. Kuhn, Jauss presents literary investigation as an analogous undertaking to procedures in the natural sciences. The study of literature, he contends, is not a process involving the gradual accumulation of facts and evidence bringing each successive generation closer to knowledge of what literature actually is or to a correct understanding of individual literary works. Rather, the development is characterized by qualitative jumps, discontinuities, and original points of departure. A paradigm that once guided literary investigation is discarded when it no longer satisfies the requirements posed for it by literary studies. A new paradigm, more suitable for this task and independent of the older model, replaces the obsolete approach until it, in turn, proves unable to cope with its function of explaining past works of literature for the present. Each paradigm defines not only the accepted methodological procedures with which critics approach literature – the "normal" literary scholarship within the academic community – but also the accepted literary canon. In other words, a given paradigm creates both the techniques for interpretation and the objects to be interpreted.

To bolster his thesis, Jauss presents a scheme in which he discusses the sequence of three previous paradigms and what he sees as the emerging paradigm in literary studies. Following a "pre-scientific" phase of literary scholarship, Jauss notes the emergence of a "classical-humanist" paradigm. This norm for literary studies involved a procedure whereby works were compared with the approved models of the ancients. Those works that successfully imitated the classics were judged good or acceptable; those that broke with the conventions of the time-honored models were bad or unsatisfactory. The task of the literary critic was to measure the works of the present against fixed rules and thus to determine whether or not they satisfied established poetic practices.

The breakdown of this paradigm in the eighteenth and nineteenth centuries is a part of the "scientific revolution" of historicism, which arose in the wake of the establishment of nation-states and the strivings for national unity throughout Europe. As a result of political changes and ideological necessities, literary history became an idealized moment of national legitimation. Consequently, activity centered on source studies, attempts to reconstruct the prehistory of standard medieval texts, and the editing of critical editions in the national tradition. The generally accepted positivistic approach of this paradigm produced the celebrated national histories of literature associated with Gervinus, Scherer, De Sanctis, and Lanson. Methodologically, this "historicist-positivist" approach is often identified with a mechanical approach to literary texts and a narrow, almost chauvinist outlook. Remnants of this paradigm exist today, Jauss notes, and he cites official government examination questions as well as the bulk of Marxist scholarship as evidence for the perseverance of this perspective. By the First World War, though, it had outlived its usefulness for productive literary research.

Out of the "growing discontent with the positivist asceticism" emerges a third paradigm, which Jauss labels "aesthetic-formalist." Associated with it are such diverse methods as the stylistic studies of Leo Spitzer and the *Geistesgeschichte* (roughly,

"history of ideas") of Oskar Walzel, as well as Russian Formalism and New Criticism. What connects these various critics and
schools is a turn from historical and causal explanations to a
concentration on the work itself. The precise description of
linguistic technique, literary devices, composition, and structure provided scholars of this paradigm with an array of interpretive tools for analysis. At the same time this approach legitimized a preoccupation with literature as such by raising the literary work to the status of a self-sufficient object for research.

The new paradigm

But since the end of the Second World War Jauss also detects
signs of the exhaustion of this paradigm. The rehabilitation of
philosophical hermeneutics, the call for criticism with more
social relevance, and the appearance of alternatives like the
archetypal criticism of Northrop Frye or structuralism are for
him symptoms of a crisis in the third paradigm. At present,
however, there are no exact indications of the precise composition of the new direction. Although structuralism – and presumably Jauss includes here varieties of "post-structuralism" as
well – may appear to be a likely candidate for the new scholarly
model, Jauss believes that its origins as an opposition to the
older philological-historical school of thought and the diversity
of critical directions that it has taken exclude it from consideration for the moment. Its primary value thus far has been its
challenge to literary scholarship to incorporate categories and
procedures developed by linguistics into the analysis of literary
works.

   Although the methodological orientation of the fourth paradigm cannot yet be determined with precision, Jauss does outline the demands that it will have to fulfill. First and foremost is the
requirement that every previous paradigm has also satisfied:
the interpretation, mediation, and actualization of past art:

> This specific accomplishment [of a literary paradigm] . . . is
> the ability to wrest works of art from the past by means of new
> interpretations, to translate them into a new present, to make
> the experiences preserved in past art accessible again; or, in
> other words, to ask the questions that are posed anew by

every generation and to which the art of the past is able to speak and again to give us answers.   (pp. 54-5)

Moreover, any new paradigm is faced with an additional challenge in contemporary society. For the increasing importance of the mass media compels any prospective paradigm to incorporate methods for dealing adequately with an entire range of hitherto unforeseen "aesthetic and quasi-aesthetic" effects. With these factors in mind, Jauss outlines three specific methodological exigencies for a fourth paradigm:

1 The mediation of aesthetic/formal and historical/ reception-related analysis, as well as art, history, and social reality;

2 The linking of structural and hermeneutical methods (which hardly take note of their respective procedures and results);

3 The probing of an aesthetics (no longer related solely to description) of effect [*Wirkung*] and a new rhetoric, which can equally well account for "high-class" literature as well as popular literature and phenomena of the mass media.   (p. 56)

Tentative steps towards the realization of such a paradigm are not entirely lacking. They can be found, Jauss claims, in the reforms initiated by the department of literature at the University of Constance, where both Jauss and Wolfgang Iser hold positions.

In this essay Jauss never mentions reception theory by name. Clearly, however, it is his favored candidate for the fourth paradigm. The two main competing theories for paradigmatic status, Marxism and structuralism, both of which made significant inroads into German academia during the late 1960s, are disqualified on rather dubious grounds. Marxism is dismissed since it is considered to consist only of mechanistic procedures; it can thus be conveniently consigned to the historicist-positivist dustbin. Structuralism, although granted a degree of legitimacy, is in the last analysis discredited because it has not exhibited the unity required for paradigmatic status. Only reception theory seems able to fulfill the three demands that Jauss postulates. And although it is never explicitly stated, the attentive reader will no doubt draw this conclusion as well.

Scientific revolutions and literary scholarship

The appropriation of Kuhn's model of scientific revolutions[1] for a history of literary scholarship also seems to be a device for enhancing the attraction of reception theory. By defining scholarly endeavor as a discontinuous enterprise, Jauss is better able to emphasize the novelty of his own efforts. Continuity with earlier attempts to elucidate the nature of aesthetic response is thereby effectively severed, and the programmatically innovative aspect of reception theory is secured. Moreover, this appropriation of the concept of a scientific revolution, in the tumultuous climate of the late 1960s at German universities, had a built-in appeal to students and younger scholars. By adopting Jauss's position on reception, they found themselves in "opposition" to the establishment and were also assured of the pioneering status of their work.

It should be noted, however, that Jauss has been forced to evade several important problems inherent in transferring Kuhn's theory. Kuhn, for example, postulates the "scientific community" as a special type of social grouping relatively independent of other organizations. He also feels that there are long periods of "normal" science, when scientists do more or less routine investigations according to established practices. During these periods there is a relative scarcity of competing paradigms. A single paradigm dominates, and it is validated and almost universally accepted by the scientific community.

Clearly these notions have limited application in literary scholarship. Literary communities – if we deign to extend this term to the literary sphere – are more often embroiled in "paradigm" controversies of a more complex nature. The continuity in Marxist criticism or in structuralist thought, the current penchant for neo-positivist methods in some European circles, or the perseverance of New Critical premises in many American universities all suggest that it is difficult to speak of a period of "normal" scholarship. No physicist would be taken seriously if he/she advocated a return to Newton. But literary scholars are still given a fair hearing when they propose phenomenological or immanent methods as the most adequate ways of interpreting texts. Looking at footnotes in scholarly works, according to Kuhn a sign of an accepted paradigm, one would be tempted to conclude that in the field of cultural studies we must speak of quasi-independent communities, each with its own paradigm, rather than a linear succession of clearly differentiated models.

The dramatic rise of reception theory

The task of this chapter is not to rewrite Jauss's sketch of the history of literary theory, nor to correct or debunk his appropriation of the paradigm model. Rather, it is to try to understand how reception theory, which was virtually unknown in 1965, could have become so popular over the next decade. To this end the discussion of how paradigms change in literary scholarship is interesting because potentially it entails the appearance of reception theory itself. Although the "Paradigm" essay may not supply a satisfactory explanation of this phenomenon, it does shed some light on how reception theory was perceived in the years of its inception: the kinds of claims, biases, and inconsistencies in Jauss's essay can be seen as indicators themselves of the way in which this "paradigm" was packaged, promoted, and consumed. In retrospect, however, it hardly seems to have required such a "hard sell." Indeed, it has proved to be one of the most marketable items that the scholarly community ever produced. Whether one thinks of its appearance as a change in paradigm or, more modestly, as a shift in emphasis, no one today can seriously question the enormous impact that reception theory has had on the interpretation of literature and art.

A few examples should serve to document the magnitude of its effect. In 1977 a bibliography of over sixty pages appeared in Gunter Grimm's *Rezeptionsgeschichte* (History of Reception);[2] most of the entries had been published during the previous decade. In the past fifteen years at least five readers or essay collections have dealt with the field of reception or reader-oriented problems. The *Zeitschrift für Literaturwissenschaft und Linguistik (LiLi)* (1974), the *Amsterdamer Beiträge zur neueren Germanistik* (1974), *Deutschunterricht* (1977), *Œuvres et Critiques* (1977–8), and *Poétique* (1979) have devoted entire issues to the topic. *Poetica* has published, in 1975 and 1976, two tentative "balance sheets" (*Zwischenbilanzen*) on the "aesthetics of reception," and the Conference of German Teachers in Stuttgart in 1972 devoted two entire sections as well as portions of others to an examination of this new development in theory. In 1979 the ninth Congress of the International Comparative Literature Association was conducted under the general title "Literary Communication and Reception," and its proceedings were published the next year in a 436-page volume.[3] In terms of concrete application to literary subjects, almost no area has been ignored. In one form or another, reception theory has been used to discuss French troubadour lyrics, the English novel tradition, the *nouveau roman*, surrealism, the *Nibelungenlied*, Lessing's *Emilia Galotti*, Goethe's *Werther*, Gerhart Hauptmann's *Weavers*, Celan's "Thread suns," Brecht's *Keuner Stories*, Grass's *Local Anaesthetic*, and a list of other topics too lengthy to enumerate here. From Marxists to traditional critics, from classical scholars and medievalists to modern specialists, virtually every methodological perspective and area of literary endeavor has responded to the challenge raised by reception theory.

Documenting the magnitude of the response among scholars and critics is easier, of course, than explaining why the response occurred. "Exhaustion" of old methods and "discontent" in general may have played a role in its rapid acceptance, but makeshift psychology of this sort inevitably raises more questions than it answers. Furthermore, it confounds symptoms with reasons. If a generation of scholars becomes disgruntled and dissatisfied with current critical practices, then these attitudes themselves are responses to, not causes for, change. The origins of this purportedly novel method must ultimately be sought within the context of German social, intellectual, and academic life during the period. It would be impossible to try to explain such an intricate development in a few sentences; but if we consider the appearance of reception theory as an answer to the methodological crisis in literary studies that arose during the 1960s, then we may be able to understand at least one facet of the interface between literary theory and the larger social sphere.

For this crisis in literary scholarship was in turn the outgrowth of a nexus of factors that penetrated almost every area of German life. At the risk of being charged with adherence to a positivist-historicist paradigm, we might explore the roots of this larger crisis with the following observations. In the economic sphere the end of the "economic miracle" and its promise of unlimited growth and prosperity as well as the first signs of recession in the middle of the decade contributed to a more questioning attitude in West Germany towards systemic and institutional structures. In the political arena, the end of the Adenauer era in 1963, the Great Coalition in 1966, and the rise to power of the SPD on a non-socialist basis are both symptoms of change and causes for further reflection (and action). It is no coincidence, for example, that the extra-parliamentary opposition (APO) finds its beginnings in this atmosphere of economic and political transformation. The list of factors that are the results of and/or the impetus for change can be easily extended. The Eichmann trial in 1960–1 and the first sustained attempts to come to terms with the Third Reich historically, the final realization with the erection of the Berlin wall that hopes for German unity were futile, the recognition that West Germany was part of an "imperialist" coalition currently conducting a brutal campaign of destruction in Vietnam, the appearance of the student movement, the maturation of the first post-war and hence post-Nazi generation – all of these played some role in the development of a new consciousness in West German society, contributing to the altered mentality of the late 1960s.

Re-evaluating methodology and the canon

The most evident manifestations of a crisis in literary studies occurred in the field of German language and literature. Reacting against both the vestiges of National Socialist methodology and the post-war introduction of non-committed, supposedly neutral scholarly practices, young academics of the 1960s attempted to rethink the possibilities for future investigations. One of the most celebrated documents of this crisis, *Ansichten einer künftigen Germanistik* (1969; Views of a Future Germanistik),[4] speaks of the field of German studies as a "much maligned discipline" and seeks to find some solution to the dominant "misery" (p. 7). The essay collection closes with a "Memorandum for the reform of the study of linguistics and literature," which proposes sweeping changes for academic programs (pp. 219–22). Not coincidentally, some of the most important critics in the first stages of reception theory – among them Jauss, Iser, and Siegfried J. Schmidt – are co-signers of this document.

The sequel to this volume, *Neue Ansichten einer künftigen Germanistik* (1973; New Views of a Future Germanistik),[5] is even more telling for the topic we are considering. The first section of contributions is grouped under the heading "Problems of a social and reception history of literature"; while the two remaining groupings, "Critique of linguistics" and "Literary scholarship and communication research," also relate in part to categories associated with reception theory. The founders of reception theory were thus involved with both the institutional and the methodological restructuring of literary studies in West Germany.

The turn to reception theory as a possible resolution to the crisis in literary methodology, documented by the second volume of *Ansichten*, is one of the most important aspects of this shift in scholarly emphasis. It is itself part of a more general concern with methodology that arose in connection with the attacks in and on academia. Young scholars began to question the hidden and not-so-hidden assumptions of their predecessors; proseminars devoted to an examination of methodological procedures became an essential element in the educational curriculum.

The academic publishing market soon experienced a flood of books dealing with approaches to literatures. Most of these methodological primers served a dual function: they were designed first to warn beginning students about the pitfalls of earlier methods and then to suggest, often in a thinly concealed undercurrent, alternatives to that tradition. The "formalist" methodology of Wolfgang Kayser's *Das sprachliche Kunstwerk* (1948; The Verbal Work of Art) and Emil Staiger's *Die Kunst der Interpretation* (1955; The Art of Interpretation)[6] were dismissed as obsolete or élitist, and the plea for reappropriating and redirecting a more historically based scholarship is apparent in the presentations. In this climate of reconsidering past practices and searching for new avenues, in this atmosphere of methodological turmoil and revolt, it is easy to understand not only why reception theory attracted such a strong following, but also why the declaration of a "scientific revolution" was a timely and apposite means of proclaiming an opposition to the status quo.

The alternative of a reception-oriented approach seemed to speak to another major consideration in literary studies as well.

As we have seen, one of Jauss's central tasks for a successful paradigm entails the mediation and reformulation of the canon. In the second half of the 1960s one begins to encounter just such a rethinking of the standard works of German literary history. Influenced partially by scholarship from the German Democratic Republic, which from its inception had harbored a quite different idea of the literary heritage, and propagated by young scholars both within and outside of West Germany, the accepted canon underwent noticeable modifications. Goethe, Schiller, and the eternal perfections associated with German classicism were confronted with the revolutionary pamphleteering and radical theater of the German Jacobins. Conservative writers from the middle of the nineteenth century, like Eduard Mörike or Adalbert Stifter, were to a large extent supplanted by the committed lyricists of the *Vormärz* or pre-1848 period. And the giants of the twentieth century, notably Franz Kafka, Rainer Maria Rilke, and Thomas Mann, had to share their literary laurels with newly discovered proletarian and socialist writers.

Authors who had been included in the old canon, albeit grudgingly and frequently with apolitical justifications, were re-examined also. Friedrich Hölderlin descended from his Heideggerian heights to Jacobin reality; Jean Paul was viewed as part of a political opposition; Georg Büchner was released from his existential pessimism and steered in the direction of the revolutionary avant-garde; and Heinrich Heine's Romantic lyrics became less important than his critical journalism and his friendship with Marx.

Reception theory claimed competence in dealing with this canonical dilemma in two ways – which often involved contradictory results. On the one hand, it represented a method for looking at the old canon anew, for re-evaluating the past and thus rescuing the old standards from this onslaught of insolent plundering. On the other hand, as Jauss makes clear in his reference to the mass media and popular literature, it provided a basis for analyzing those works that had been traditionally excluded from selection, as well as the reasons for these omissions. And in the context of these struggles over an acceptable canon, the promise of a revised and continuously revisable canon was a not insignificant part of its appeal.

Connections with contemporary literature

Perhaps more important than the promise to renew the past, however, was the ability to relate to the present. Reception theory was not remiss in this area either. If we conceive of reception theory as a general redirecting of attention to the pole of the reader or audience, then several parallels between German literature of the 1960s and the shift in critical perspectives are apparent. The rise of documentary literature is perhaps the most obvious example. From Rolf Hochhuth's *The Deputy* (1963) to Heinar Kipphardt's *In the Matter of J. Robert Oppenheimer* (1964) or Peter Weiss's *The Investigation* (1965), one observes a development from a concern with production and presentation to a concentration on effect and response. In one documentary drama, in fact, Hans Magnus Enzensberger's *The Hearing of Havanna* (1970), members of the audience were involved in discussions after the performance, and the entire evening was broadcast on national television. The intention was to maximize both audience involvement and effect. In addition, one could point to two early plays by Peter Handke, *Offending the Audience* (1966) and *Kaspar* (1967), both of which attempt to break down traditional barriers between viewer and stage action with a variety of unconventional techniques.

The novel of the era also exhibits a growing concern with reader response. For the sake of brevity two examples will have to suffice, *Efraim* (1967) by the Swiss novelist Alfred Andersch and *Jakob the Liar* (1968) by the East German author Jurek Becker. Both were fairly popular works and roughly contemporaneous with the initial manifestos of reception theory. In *Efraim* Andersch tries to engage the reader by a number of devices including specific and frequent references to the "presumed reader." Becker toys with reader expectations by providing two endings to his narrative: the first, a happy ending, which did not occur, and the second, the actual course of events, which leads the main character to the gas chamber. Both works, in short, incorporate the reader into the narrative structure by anticipating responses and reflecting on the traditional ways in which texts communicate with an anonymous audience.

Structural changes in the literature of the 1960s, like any other isolated factor, cannot explain the rise of reception theory.

At most the preceding outline of social, scholarly, and literary considerations can provide some insight into the climate that made a change in method possible. Rather than supplying causes for which reception theory is the inevitable consequence, the various aspects of German social life constitute the conditions of possibility for the formulation, acceptance, and popularity of this purportedly new perspective in literary studies. "Methods," Jauss notes at the beginning of his "Paradigm" essay, "do not fall from the sky, but have their place in history" (p. 45). Reception theory is no exception to this rule. It developed in a conflict-ridden situation in German literary and political life and consequently took its place on the critical scene in a complex dialogue and debate with other methods and traditions. It not only had to fend off competing tendencies by declaring them obsolete or incomplete, but also had to assume the posture, especially in its initial phases, of rebellion and novelty.

In retrospect, Jauss's "Paradigm" essay can itself be judged paradigmatic – in a manner he would never have suspected at the time of its composition. For in the context of the late 1960s it appears as the prototype of a scholarly manifesto. Utilizing rhetoric as much as logic, it seeks to persuade by analogy, rather than coherent argument. By adopting Kuhn's popular theory of scholarly change, it sets up a "plot" whose outcome must be favorable to reception theory. By none the less refusing to name this outcome, it endeavors to convince the reader that he/she is freely arriving at the correct conclusion. And by implicitly presenting reception theory as the resolution to a crisis and a "scientific revolution," it simultaneously suggests a return to normalcy and an overthrow of existing dogma. Like so many of the theoretical manifestos of that era, it too might have been long forgotten if the method it promoted had not turned out to be precisely the answer that German scholarship sought. In spite of its contradictions and confusions, then, Jauss's "Paradigm" essay, itself a paradigm in its genre, has turned out to bear more legitimacy than its argumentation might seem to allow.

Influences
and precursors

The emergence of a new approach to literature, especially one that claims paradigmatic status, inevitably generates a series of studies that explore roots and thereby tarnish claims to originality. In a certain sense one might say that a theory creates its own forerunners, and this maxim can be applied to reception theory as well. Indeed, in the years immediately following its appearance, several investigations have sought to demonstrate its dependence on earlier thought. In a general sense precursors are not difficult to find. Aristotle's *Poetics*, by its inclusion of catharsis as a central category of aesthetic experience, may be considered the earliest illustration of a theory in which audience response plays a major role. In fact, the entire tradition of rhetoric and its relationship to poetic theory can likewise be viewed as a precursor by virtue of its focus on the impact of oral and written communication on the listener or reader. In the German tradition, Lessing's exegesis of Aristotelian categories is perhaps the best-known example of a theoretical departure in which the effect that a drama exerts on the individual viewer is accorded substantial emphasis. In a larger sense, however, the entire aesthetic tradition of the eighteenth century, from its beginnings as a separate branch of philosophical enquiry in Baumgarten's 1750 treatise *Aesthetica* to Kant's *Critique of Judgment* (1790), relies on notions of what the artwork does as much as what it is.

"Precursors" to or "anticipators" of reception theory can thus be uncovered without much effort. Establishing influence, however, is a bit more complex, involving principles, no doubt, developed by reception theory itself. The reason for the appropriation of a given theory at a particular time in a particular fashion is not simply a matter of the availability of material. The editorial policies of publishing houses or the selections of libraries may very well have some effect on the development of theory, but they are never enough to determine impact. There must, in addition, be some readiness on the part of the intellectual community to rethink its methods, and this preparedness coupled with an influx of theoretical impulses may then lead to a productive reception. What are labeled influences or precursors in this chapter, therefore, are those theories or tendencies that appeared or reappeared during the 1960s and that defined an intellectual climate in which reception theory could flourish.

Five influences have been marked for precursor status on this basis: Russian Formalism, Prague structuralism, the phenomenology of Roman Ingarden, Hans-Georg Gadamer's hermeneutics, and the "sociology of literature." They were selected either because they have had a noticeable impact on theoretical developments, as evidenced in the footnotes or sources of leading reception theorists, or because they have contributed to solutions to the crisis in literary scholarship discussed above by refocusing attention on the text–reader relationship. In most cases there is a direct influence on the theorists of the so-called Constance School, a designation used here to refer not only to those who teach and were taught at the University of Constance, but also to the frequent contributors to the biannual colloquia held there since the mid-1960s. Restricting attention largely to the precursors to this group is justified because its members have had the most impact on shaping the international reputation of reception theory and because this school seems to be responsible for the principles that sparked this critical direction in divergent circles. Certainly Marxist or empiricist variants of reception theory could point to other significant influences, and some of the work included under the unavoidably vague rubric "sociology of literature" undoubtedly contributed to these modes of studying reception. But since the Constance School has made reception theory a phenomenon in modern German literary scholarship, its precursors merit a more thorough review.

The criteria used to select "precursors" – the promulgation during the 1960s and evidence of impact – must be accompanied by two warnings. First, the theories discussed below cannot be treated in their entirety. Each contains an abundance of views on literature and art that extend well beyond the scope of this chapter. Only those particular aspects that relate to reception theory or contributed to an altered perspective in literary investigation will receive extensive treatment. Second, the following survey makes no claims for completeness even as it relates to the Constance School. Many works have been excluded, either because their influence has been restricted to a small branch of literary scholarship or because they themselves are less directly concerned with matters of literature. What is included, in short, are the theories that dominated the literary scene during the late 1960s and early 1970s, i.e. the most frequently quoted works with aesthetic or literary import.

Russian Formalism

The impact of Formalism

The claim that Russian Formalism contributed heavily to the development of reception theory may seem puzzling to the Anglo-American reader. For in the English-speaking world this important movement of the early twentieth century has been associated more often with either New Criticism or structuralism. These associations are not unfounded. The Formalists' concern with the composition of literary works and their careful analyses of rhyme and poetic form seem to ally them with the New Critics, who likewise paid close attention to textual analysis. And the dependence on linguistic features of texts as well as the more general concerns with the nature of language have led to an identification between Russian Formalism and Parisian structuralism. Indeed, this latter connection is one both the structuralists themselves and the explicators of structuralism have repeatedly stressed.

Yet the importance of Russian Formalism for German criticism of the late 1960s is also difficult to overlook. Although one cannot deny the affinities between the Formalists and both New Criticism and French structuralism, a somewhat different image of this school emerges from the German perspective of the 1970s. What is important in Germany is not so much the concentration on the work of art or the linguistic roots and ramifications, but rather the shift in vantage point to the text–reader relationship. By widening the concept of form to include aesthetic perception, by defining the work of art as the sum of its "devices," and by directing attention to the process of interpretation itself, the Russian Formalists contribute to a novel manner of exegesis closely related to reception theory. With respect to literary history the Formalist postulate of "literary evolution," involving the struggle for supremacy of different schools, has strong echoes in recent German theory as well. Indeed, most German observers have no trouble in connecting these early Russian theorists with their native concerns. One is forced to conclude, then, that next to the structuralist lineage from Moscow to Paris there is a parallel succession in the history of ideas running from the Formalists to modern German reception theorists.

Perception and the "device"

The shift in attention from the pole of author–work to the relationship between text and reader is perhaps exhibited most clearly in the early writings of Viktor Shklovskii. In his polemic against Alexander Potebnia's apothegm "art is thinking in images," he has almost immediate recourse to principles of perception (I, pp. 3–35).[1] Imagery is not the constitutive element of literature, according to Shklovskii, for it is itself only a means of creating the strongest possible impression, one of many poetic devices used to maximize effect. In an examination of art one should not start with symbols or metaphor, themselves instruments for effect, but rather with general laws of perception. And it is in this area that Shklovskii discovers the guiding principles for analyzing and evaluating works of art. For him, ordinary perception, which is associated with practical language, tends to become habitual or automatic. The "algebrization" or "making automatic" of perception leads inevitably to a failure to "see" the object; instead, one merely recognizes it, i.e. perceives it in a habitual fashion.

The function of art, on the other hand, is to dehabitualize our perception, to make the object come alive again. The role of the recipient is thus of primary importance; in a certain sense it is the perceiver who determines the artistic quality of the work. For an object can be created as prosaic and perceived as poetic, or, conversely, created as poetic and perceived as prosaic.

> This shows that the artistry attributed to the poetry of a given object is the result of our perception; artistic objects, in the narrow sense, are those that are created with special devices whose purpose is that these objects, with the greatest possible certainty, be perceived as artistic. (I, pp. 6–7)

Despite the circularity of definition, the general meaning is clear. Only those objects that are perceived as artistic, as deviations from habitual and automatized perceptions, merit the adjective "artistic." Perception and not creation, reception, not production, become the constituent elements of art.

From this epistemologico-aesthetic foundation, which was shared to a large degree by the early Formalists, it is easy to comprehend why the "device" became a central tool for literary analysis. For the device is the means by which we become aware of objects, the technique which makes the thing perceivable and artistic. For this reason Roman Jakobson, in a lecture on contemporary Russian poetry given in 1919, places this concept at the very heart of literary interpretation (II, pp. 18–35). Since the object of literary scholarship is not literature, but "literariness" (*literaturnost'*), that is, the quality which makes a work literary, and since literariness is defined in terms of devices, one could not escape the conclusion that concern with the device was the task of criticism. "If literary scholarship wishes to become a science, then it needs to accept the 'device' as its only 'hero'" (II, pp. 30–3).

The meaning and application of this concept seem to have varied widely among various Formalist practitioners, however. In the address quoted above, Jakobson subsumes the play with suffixes, the proximity of two unities (parallelism, comparison, metaphor), and a variety of other linguistic features under the rubric "device." Boris Eikhenbaum, in an analysis of Gogol's

Overcoat, speaks of the chief device of the *skaz* (I, pp. 134–5) and aims at elucidating the type of linking of the individual devices (I, pp. 146–7). And Jurii Tynianov warns against a static consideration of the device. Its importance does not lie in its mere existence, but rather in its function in the process of literary evolution (I, pp. 402–3). There are three factors which appear to unite these rather disparate uses of the term. First, the device is considered exclusively as a formal element, the manner of constructing the work of art; its domain is composition rather than content. Second, it functions against a specific background, whether this be practical language or the literary tradition. Finally, and most important for our present concerns, it is the element that bridges the gap between text and reader, making the work itself a worthwhile and genuine aesthetic object.

Defamiliarization

It is Shklovskii's concept of defamiliarization, however, which is most often associated with the device. Indeed, from his early essays it is difficult to ascertain whether defamiliarization is a type of device or its defining characteristic. In either case *ostranenie* ("making strange") refers to a particular relationship between reader and text that removes the object from its normal perceptive field. And in this sense it is the constitutive element in all art:

> The device of art is the device of "defamiliarization" of objects and the device of the form made difficult, a device that increases the difficulty and length of perception; for the process of perception is in art an end in itself and must be prolonged. (I, pp. 14–15)

In a series of illustrations from Tolstoy, Shklovskii proceeds to explain how this device has been applied. Tolstoy defamiliarizes flogging by description and by the proposal to change its form without changing its essence; in *Khlostomer* he allows a horse to narrate, thereby indicting the institution of private property; and in *War and Peace* battles are portrayed in a strange light to heighten perception (I, pp. 16–23).

There are really two functions of defamiliarization operative in these examples. On the one hand, these devices illuminate linguistic and social conventions, forcing the reader to see them in a new and critical light: although Shklovskii does not appear to draw any consequences from this method of exposing injustice, this aspect certainly comes closest to what Bertolt Brecht meant by the "estrangement effect." On the other hand, the device serves to draw attention to the form itself. In a sense it compels the reader to ignore the social ramifications by directing attention to the process of defamiliarization as an element of art. What is most important from the perspective of reception theory, though, is that Shklovskii is here formulating a rudimentary component of the reading process. Defamiliarization, though intended by the author for manipulative or perceptive purposes, is a process that establishes a relationship between reader and text, and literature as art is defined by this very activity.

The focus on the device of defamiliarization quite naturally led the Formalists to a concern for those authors or movements consciously seeking to expose the nature of literature by "laying bare the device" (*obnazhenie priema*). Avant-garde poets, satirists, and parodists are particularly important in this regard, for the function of their writing is to make the reader conscious of the work *qua* art. The laying bare of the device might be viewed as defamiliarization raised to the second power. While the latter technique merely exposes various conventions, redirecting attention to the form itself, the former reveals the very devices in their function of constituting art. Thus Jakobson has recourse to this concept in his discussion of the futurist poets Vladimir Maiakovskii and Viktor Khlebnikov; by playing with conventions in an unusual fashion, both lyricists make technique itself visible (II, pp. 32–3; 58–9). Similar thoughts occur in Shklovskii's celebrated investigation of *Tristram Shandy* (I, pp. 244–99). Sterne, a "revolutionary of form," distinguishes himself from his predecessors in that he presents artistic form as such, outside of any motivation. That Shklovskii finds parallels between Sterne's efforts and those of the futurists and that he can assert that *Tristram Shandy* is "the most typical novel in world literature" are simply the logical results of the Formalist theory of device.

It was Tynianov, though, who arrived at a more differentiated and evolutionary view of *obnazhenie priema*. He recognized that exposing the device could itself become automatized, as it had, in fact, with Sterne's epigones in the late eighteenth century. What would be necessary in such a case, then, is a reconcealing of the device; only in this manner could one account for the dynamic character of literary history (I, pp. 408–9). But here, too, Tynianov relies on an orientation consonant with the theory of reception. While he corrects Shklovskii's notion of *obnazhenie priema*, he still depends on the perception of the work of art. The device must be hidden only when the reader has realized the habitual nature of its exposure.

The significance of the reader's role in the literary process extends beyond attention to the formal nature of the device. A case in point is Boris Tomashevskii's essay, "Literature and biography."[2] Considering the Formalists' rejection of traditional scholarship with its dependence on the "life-and-work" method, we would expect biography in particular to be banished from critical studies. But this is so only when the scholar uses it to illuminate the life of the author. It is not true, Tomashevskii suggests, when one examines it for its literary function. The relationship of biography to literature is not a question of the genesis or description of the work, but rather of its reception. "Before we can answer this question, however, we must remember that creative literature exists, not for literary historians, but for readers, and we must consider how the poet's biography operates in the reader's consciousness" (p. 47). While the actual biography or curriculum vitae may be interesting as a cultural phenomenon, only the legend of the author's life, the "ideal biography," is important for the literary historian. The reader's image of Pushkin, Rousseau, or Voltaire, for example, is instrumental in an interpretation and evaluation of their works. To be sure, not all authors, even those who do not remain anonymous in the strict sense of the word, have relevant biographies. "There are writers with biographies and writers without biographies" (p. 55), Tomashevskii asserts; that is, "eras during which the personality of the artist was of no interest at all to the audience" (p. 47). Only with the advent of "the individualization of creativity" (p. 48) do the name and personality of the author play a role in our perception. But in these cases the legend created by the author (and, one might add, created by future generations) becomes a "*literary fact*" (p. 55). An adequate reading of a given writer is, therefore, not solely dependent on analyzing formal devices; from the reader's perspective, the ideal biography is an essential mediating element between text and audience.

Literary evolution

There is one additional area in which Formalist theory has had a considerable impact on reception theory, namely, literary history. For the Formalists, the notion of a progression in art can be seen as an outgrowth and application of the concept of device. Since the device is defined by Shklovskii in terms of its ability to defamiliarize perceptions and since what is familiar is determined to some extent by current literary practice, changes in art are brought about by a rejection of the contemporary artistic modes. The result is, as Fredric Jameson has noted, an "artistic permanent revolution,"[3] a succession of generations or schools which each in turn replaces stale techniques with striking and provocative formal innovations.

The political metaphor, however, fails to capture one important aspect of Formalist literary history. A continuity can be established in this "revolutionary" process, and it does not consist solely in the negation of one's predecessors. Shklovskii stresses that a new school of literature inevitably relies on a forgotten or non-dominant heritage for its basic principles. The inheritance, according to him, is not patrilineal, but rather avuncular. Literary history, then, does "progress," but in a broken rather than a straight line. In practice, Shklovskii concedes, matters are not so simple.

> The new hegemony is usually not a pure instance of a restoration of earlier form, but one involving the presence of features from other junior schools, even features (but now in a subordinate role) inherited from its predecessors on the throne.[4]

But in general the "*dialectical self-production of new forms*"[5] defines the nature of literary history and accounts for the rise and fall of literary schools.

Tynianov, once again, goes a long way towards refining the somewhat one-sided view of Shklovskii. His contribution to a theory of literary history, like his views on "laying bare the device," may be seen as a corrective to Shklovskii's overstate-

ments, although it should be noted that he shares most fundamental tenets with his Formalist compatriot. He appears to
retain, for example, both the notion of formal innovation as the
decisive element in literary history (and thus the inner-literary
nature of the entire process) and the proposition of development
by leaps and struggles. By 1929, however, in his important essay
"On literary evolution" he adopts two theses which take him far
beyond Shklovskii's theory (I, pp. 432–61). The first involves
the systemic and functional quality of literature. By introducing
these notions, he is able to conceive of literary evolution as the
"replacement of systems" (I, pp. 436–7), and by distinguishing
between auto-functions (those interrelated in a literary system)
and syn-functions (those interrelated in a single work) he can
explain in a more differentiated fashion the various struggles,
replacements, distortions, and parodies which characterize
changes in artistic technique.

The second notion, which grows out of this functional
approach, concerns the term "dominant." It signifies the element or group of elements that is placed in the foreground in a
given work or during a given period. Succession in literary
history can then be viewed as a continuous replacement of one
group of dominants by another. They do not drop out of the
system entirely; rather they recede into the background to
reappear later in a novel manner. The fecundity of this explanation for reception theory is apparent. It helps to account for not
only the changes in the literary canon, but also the shift in
critical emphasis when judging the "great" works of literature
during different periods. If a given work is sufficiently rich in
interpretive potential, a change in dominants will simply result
in the recognition and praise of hitherto unnoticed features. As
we shall see shortly, these notions of the dynamics of literary
history have implications for both Jauss's "horizon of expectations" and Iser's "gaps" and "indeterminacies."

Roman Ingarden

Ingarden's reception

The fate of Roman Ingarden's work has been as varied as that of
the Russian Formalists; indeed, it would itself provide an

interesting case study for reception theory. As a student of Edmund Husserl involved primarily with questions of philosophy, Ingarden took up the problems of literary works of art out of these more theoretical concerns. As he himself wrote in 1930, the literary work of art presented him with the perfect case of

> an object whose pure intentionality was beyond any doubt and on the basis of which one could study the essential structures of the mode of existence of the purely intentional object without being subject to suggestions stemming from considerations of real objectivities.[1]

His ultimate motive for turning to the study of literary theory is directly related to the examination of the problematic of idealism and realism, since according to Ingarden the literary work of art falls outside of this dichotomy; the subtitle of *The Literary Work of Art, An Investigation on the Borderlines of Ontology, Logic, and Theory of Literature*, underscores this philosophical aim.

But the two most important responses to Ingarden's work, while not denying his phenomenological ties, tend to play down his chief philosophical concerns. René Wellek's reception of Ingarden, for example, brings him into association with principles of New Criticism. Although his name appears only sparingly in *Theory of Literature* (1946),[2] it is clear that his work was important for Wellek's thinking, especially his discussion of the "mode of existence" of the literary work. What connects Ingarden's work with Wellek and ultimately with the entire Anglo-American New Critical movement is less the realism–idealism issue than his insistence on analyzing literature intrinsically; the New Critics and Ingarden share the view that the work itself should be the focal point of investigation. The pervasiveness of this methodological dictum, especially Wellek's role in promoting it, bears witness to the significance of this side of his reception.

Another dimension of Ingarden's theory, however, has made itself evident in Germany during the past decade and a half. While his earlier impact in Germany had also been related to the "intrinsic" approach, more recently Ingarden has become known for his study of the reading process and the cognition of literary works. To some extent the divergence in impact is the result of the reception of two different works. While Wellek and the New Critics drew their knowledge from *The Literary Work of Art*, the German publication of *The Cognition of the Literary Work of Art* in 1968 allowed prospective reception theorists to see more clearly Ingarden's concern with the relationship between the text and the reader.[3] Neither the New Critics nor reception theorists, though, appear to have been interested in the larger philosophical issues that attracted Ingarden to his subject.

The structure of indeterminacy

The most influential segment of Ingarden's work for recent German criticism, his analysis of cognition, is based upon his conception of the literary artwork. He considers the literary work to be a purely intentional or heteronomous object, i.e. one which is neither determinate nor autonomous (as both real and ideal objects are), but rather dependent on an act of consciousness. It consists of four layers or strata, each of which affects the others, and two distinct dimensions. In the first layer, comprising the "raw material" of literature, the "word-sounds" (*Wortlaute*) and those phonetic formations built upon them, we find not only the sound configurations that carry meanings, but also the potential for special aesthetic effects such as rhythm and rhyme. The second stratum includes all meaning units (*Bedeutungseinheiten*), whether they are words, sentences, or units composed of multiple sentences. The third and fourth layers consist of represented objects (*dargestellte Gegenstände*) and the schematized aspects (*schematisierte Ansichten*) by which these objects appear. The totality of these four strata, this first dimension of the literary work of art, brings about a polyphonic harmony that Ingarden associates with aesthetic value. The second, temporal dimension comprises the sequence of sentences, paragraphs, and chapters that are contained in the literary work.

What is particularly important for Ingarden's theory of cognition of the literary work is the notion that these layers and dimensions form a skeleton or "schematized structure" to be completed by the reader. This is most easily observed with the third and fourth strata, which deal with represented objects. In contrast to real objects, which are "*unequivocally, universally* (i.e. in *every* respect) *determined*" (*Literary Work*, p. 246) – there are no places where such objects would not be in themselves totally determined – the objects represented in a literary work exhibit "spots" or "points" or "places" of indeterminacy (*Unbestimmtheitsstellen*). "We find such a place of indeterminacy," Ingarden writes, "wherever it is impossible, on the basis of the sentences in the work, to say whether a certain object or objective situation has a certain attribute" (*Cognition*, p. 50).

All objects, according to phenomenological theory, have an infinite number of determinants, and no act of cognition can take into account every determinant of any particular object. But while a real object must have a *particular* determinant – a real object cannot be merely colored; it must have a particular color – the objects in a literary work, because they are intentionally projected from meaning units and aspects, must retain some degree of indeterminacy. For example, if we read the sentence, "The child bounced the ball," we are confronted with a myriad of "gaps" in the represented object. Whether the child in this case is 10 or 6 years old, whether it is male or female, brown or white, red-haired or blond – all of these features are not contained in this sentence and thus constitute "gaps" or points of indeterminacy. Every child must have an age, a sex, a skin color, and a hair color, but even if the sentence in question or following sentences stipulated these attributes of the child, others would necessarily remain unspecified or indeterminate. It is possible, of course, for the text to restrict or at least to suggest limitations on the scope of the indeterminacy without mentioning particulars. If the sentence above had occurred in a novel whose setting was Sweden, we might be inclined to imagine the child as a blond Caucasian. But there is no amount of detail or suggestion that would eliminate all indeterminacy. In theory, then, each literary work, indeed, each represented object or aspect, contains an infinite number of indeterminate places.

Concretization and concretion

Now during the reading process we interact with the literary work in a variety of ways. According to Ingarden our cognition plays an active part with respect to all layers of the work. The stratum of word-sounds may become manifest through recitation or merely through realizing the sounds and sound con-figurations in silent reading. In a like manner individual read-ings, if they are at all competent, can hardly avoid actualizing a good portion of the meaning units. Gaps in the temporal structure (the so-called second dimension of the work) also need to be bridged for the text to be comprehensible.

But perhaps the most important activity readers undertake involves removing or filling out the indeterminacies, gaps, or schematized aspects in the text. Ingarden usually refers to this activity as concretization, although he also uses the term, especially in *The Literary Work of Art*, to distinguish the apprehended literary work from its skeletal structure, the aes-thetic object from the artefact. In the narrower sense concretiza-tion refers to any "complementing determination," any initia-tive taken by the reader to fill in a place of indeterminacy (*Cognition*, p. 53). Although this activity is often unconscious, for Ingarden at least it is an essential part of apprehending a literary work of art; without concretizations the aesthetic work with its presented world would not emerge from the schematic structure.[4] But in concretizing, readers also have the opportu-nity to exercise their phantasy. Filling in indeterminate places requires creativity and, Ingarden indicates, skill and perspi-cuity as well. Moreover, since concretizations are considered the activity of individual readers, they can be subject to vast variation. Personal experiences, moods, and a whole array of other contingencies can affect each concretization. Thus no two concretizations are ever precisely identical, even when they are the product of the same reader.

In a larger sense, Ingarden employs the word concretization to designate the result of actualizing the potentialities, objectify-ing the sense-units, and concretizing the indeterminacies in a given text. It occurs, he writes, when aspects attain concrete-ness and "are raised to the level of perceptual experience (in the case of a play) or imaginational experience (in a reading)" (*Literary Work*, p. 339). To avoid confusion we might refer to concretization in this usage as the "concretion" of a work.

Now Ingarden is careful not to equate a concretion with the apprehension of a work or with a psychic state. Although a concretion is "conditioned in its existence by corresponding experiences" in the reader, it is codetermined by the literary work. With respect to the experience of apprehension, therefore, a concretion "is just as transcendent as the literary work itself" (*Literary Work*, p. 336). But while the number of concretions of any work is infinite, the work itself is invariable. Ingarden thus draws a sharp theoretical distinction between the stable structure of a work and what the reader does in realizing this structure.

Moreover, while concretizing a literary work may involve an aesthetic experience, this is only one alternative of possible literary experiences. Ingarden distinguishes first between the non- or extra-aesthetic experience – he gives the example of a classical scholar reading the *Iliad* to teach the customs of the ancient Greeks – and the aesthetic experience itself. Furthermore, he comments at length on two more scholarly modes of relating to a literary work: a pre-aesthetic cognition of the work and an aesthetic reflective cognition of a concretion. (*Cognition*, p. 221–3). Ingarden associates the latter with evaluation. The former scholarly activity, which results in a "reconstruction" of the literary work, consists in investigating the skeletal structure of the work and establishing the "artistic values" that make concretions and, in genuine literary works, aesthetic values possible. In theory scholars should be able to reach agreement on the reconstruction of the literary work of art.

Determinacy, adequate concretization, and metaphysical qualities

It is at this point, however, that we should begin to object to Ingarden's system. Even if we agree with him that concretions of a given work must differ from reader to reader and even from reading to reading, why should we be inclined to think that absolute agreement is possible with respect to the structures that allow these concretions? Although we might concede that some stable structure exists – indeed, on the level of graphic marks on a page it is difficult to get around this conclusion – it does not follow that this structure is completely identifiable, definable in the terms that Ingarden dictates ("spots of indeterminacy"), or immune to the same types of contingencies that affect concretization. If indeterminacy is always infinite in a text, it is difficult to conceive of the theoretical agreement Ingarden desires, even when the "cool, analytical procedure" he advocates is applied. One has the impression here that faced with an empirically verifiable indeterminacy at the level of concretions and evaluations (*de gustibus non est disputandum*) Ingarden simply shifts determinacy from the level of concretions to the level of the schematized structure. While this shift may solve the theoretical issue of variance in interpretation and taste, it only brings us closer to determinate statements about a text in the realm of pure theory.

The advocacy of this skeletal level of determinacy has more telling implications for Ingarden's notion of the literary work of art and the reader's activity. Since the gaps and indeterminacies can be described with precision, Ingarden feels that it ought to be possible to determine boundaries for concretizations as well. Thus he postulates that there are adequate and inadequate concretizations. And although this distinction itself is not altogether objectionable – especially if we are somehow to limit outlandish and arbitrary interpretations – the way in which Ingarden associates adequate concretizations with conventional literary norms represents a serious problem for his theory.

One can trace Ingarden's normative or "classical" bias back to the description of the work of art itself. Although at times he endeavors to incorporate more modern literary movements, e.g. expressionism, into his theoretical framework, the preponderance of conventional terminology and examples from the traditional canon suggests a neglect, if not the total exclusion, of non-realistic, non-mimetic, experimental works. Ingarden's literary work of art is repeatedly associated with such loaded terms as "harmony," "polyphony," "crystallization center," or "unity"; in short, with concepts that define individual works and the whole of literature in terms of traditional poetics.

This tendency towards postulating a "classical" norm for the work and its reception is most evident in Ingarden's discussion of metaphysical qualities (*Literary Work*, pp. 290–9). His conviction that "the literary work of art attains its high point in the manifestation of metaphysical qualities" (*Literary Work*, p. 294) has drastic consequences for both the conception of literature and the reader's role. On the one hand, it leads Ingarden to hypothesize an "organic unity" for the work despite the stratified structure, and the strata, in turn, "must cooperate

harmoniously in a determinate way and fulfill specific conditions" (*Literary Work*, p. 298). On the other hand, the metaphysical qualities become the controlling forces in the reader's
concretion: inadequacy of concretion becomes equated with an
inability or unwillingness on the reader's part to realize the
work as a totality with concomitant metaphysical qualities.

Ingarden thus conceives of his reader as an ideal individual,
divorced from and independent of any larger collectivity. Questions of politics or issues of class are viewed only as hindrances
to concretization and are as unwelcome and avoidable as
inattentiveness to the text. The chief weakness of Ingarden's
phenomenological perspective thus has less to do with his
insistence on an adequate concretion of the text than with his
failure to account for the always situated nature of both the work
of art and its recipient. As we shall see presently, however, this
fundamental weakness was precisely what was avoided in the
turn to semiology by the theorists of the Prague School.

Prague structuralism (Jan Mukařovský and Felix Vodička)

Like the writings of the Russian Formalists, the work of Jan
Mukařovský, the most important literary theorist from the
Prague Structuralist School, was almost unknown in Germany
before the late 1960s. In fact, aside from a few essays in French
and German written during the 1930s, westerners in general
have had no access to his major achievements until relatively
recently. In the English-speaking world the deleterious effects of
this underexposure extend to the present day. Despite the
recent publication of two volumes of essays in English,
Mukařovský has not achieved anywhere near the attention he
merits.[1] Even those instrumental in promoting French structuralism, in many respects the intellectual heir to the Prague
School, have demonstrated little concern for his work.

In Germany, by contrast, Mukařovský's work in particular
became one of the most dominant theoretical forces during the
late 1960s and early 1970s. Between 1967 and 1974 many of his
most important writings appeared in German translation.
Moreover, his work immediately became the focus of critical
discussions from a variety of perspectives. Whenever reception

theory or structuralism were mentioned in Germany during these years, a reference to Mukařovský was almost certain.

Critique of Formalism

This popularity may have been due in part to the perception of Mukařovský as a continuator of the Russian Formalist tradition, particularly in those areas in which he develops further the reception-oriented aspects of this critical school. Up until the early 1930s he seems to have accepted the basic tenets of Formalist doctrine: he, too, apparently felt that literary analysis must never go beyond the boundaries set by the work itself. Yet by the mid-1930s his theoretical outlook had shifted noticeably; he began to recognize that an internal analysis of the text, or even a consideration of evolutionary literary history like Tynianov's, was inadequate for dealing with the complexity of the literary work, especially the relationship between literature and society.

In an essay written in 1934 on the occasion of the publication of the Czech translation of Shklovskii's *Theory of Prose*, we can witness Mukařovský's cautious, but principled objections to his Formalist predecessor (*Word*, pp. 134–42). He is first careful to note the necessity of Formalism, apologizing for Shklovskii's occasional "one-sidedness" by recalling the state of literary criticism when he wrote. Formalism, Mukařovský claims, was only "a militant slogan" that Shklovskii adopted to combat traditional literary theory. Moreover, Formalism never really existed in any strict sense of the word; "it did not correspond to reality even at the time it was accepted as a formulation of a program" (*Word*, p. 136). Mukařovský thus rescues parts of Shklovskii's work not only by arguing that his theory was a historical necessity, but also by contending that the genuine accomplishments of the Formalists were not really Formalist at all. Indeed, Mukařovský claims that "Shklovskii tended toward structuralism from the beginning" (*Word*, p. 137). By understanding the structure of the artwork as a complex semantic composition, by destroying the insidious antinomy of form and content, Shklovskii had taken the first steps towards clarifying the semiotic nature of art. "Pure" Formalism, which recognizes only the internal and autonomous development of literature, is the antithesis of traditional criticism with its emphasis on a solely external dynamic. But what Mukařovský detects in Shklovskii's work and what he himself will place at the center of his theory is the interpenetration of social reality and literary text. Structuralism, Mukařovský concludes, represents the overcoming of the Formalist–traditionalist opposition.

Art as a signifying system

Mukařovský's suggestiveness for reception theory is most evident when he outlines his conception of art as a dynamic signifying system. According to this conception, each individual work of art is a structure, but one that has references to what has preceded it inhering in its very essence. Structures are thus not independent of history, but formed and determined by a diachronic series. Nor are they limited in size or scope. The individual work is only one example of a structure; potentially, any author's *œuvre*, contemporary art forms, and even national or international literature can be studied structurally as well (*Structure*, pp. 3–16). Moreover, structures should not be conceived as independent, self-sufficient entities. Changes in any single structure – e.g. the discovery of a lost work by an author – will necessarily alter the perception of other, related structures.

But what is perhaps more important about these structures is that they act as signs. In fact, Mukařovský designates the artwork itself as a complex sign, a "semiotic fact" that mediates between the artist and the addressee (audience, listener, reader, etc.) (*Structure*, pp. 82–8). By viewing the artwork from this semiotic perspective, he is able to dismiss both the psychologizing theories that identified art with the artist's or the perceiving subject's state of mind as well as theories that treat art merely as a reflection of social reality. And with these two hindrances removed, the work of art is placed in a propitious context for examining aesthetic response. Mukařovský initiates such an investigation by looking more closely at the semiotic character of the artwork, which according to him functions in two ways: both as a communicative sign and as an autonomous structure. In its communicative aspect it is likened to *parole* (i.e. the actual manifestation of speech in a given language system). Mukařovský cautions, however, that the *entire* work should be understood as the "message"; it should not be seen as a "content" enclosed in a meaningless container or "form." As an autonomous structure Mukařovský divides the artwork into three components: a work-thing (*dílo-věc*) or artefact, the sensory symbol that corresponds in Saussure's terminology to the *signifiant* (signifier); "an 'aesthetic-object' lodged in the social consciousness and functioning as 'meaning'" (*Structure*, p. 88) (*signifié* or signified); and a relation to the thing signified, the referential aspect of the sign.

Although both functions of the artwork incorporate the recipient into the analytical framework and thus contribute to a reception-oriented perspective, the second component of the artwork in its autonomous function is perhaps the most suggestive for literary theory. For the emphasis on social consciousness points to the area that distinguishes Mukařovský from both Ingarden, who likewise separates the artefact from its aesthetic concretion, and the Russian Formalists, for whom societal realities were unwelcome intruders on critical terrain.

In Mukařovský's theory the perceiving subject is not seen as an autonomous, idealized individual; he is neither an abstract, phenomenological subject nor an ideal perceiver thoroughly acquainted with literary history. Rather, the recipient is him/herself a product of social relations. Although Mukařovský continues to use the singular form of "viewer" or "perceiver" in his writings, he stresses the collective process involved in the reception of art. Thus in his seminal essay of 1936, *Aesthetic Function, Norm and Value as Social Facts*, he affirms the social nature of both the sign and the recipient.[2] By considering the artwork to be a social sign and its viewer a "social creature, a member of a collective" (*Aesthetic Function*, p. 83), Mukařovský avoids aesthetic subjectivism as well as the idealizing tendencies of the phenomenologist and Formalist positions. His semiology, in other words, is able to incorporate sociology, not by positing the mechanistic reflection of an already constituted reality, but by presupposing the prior penetration of reality into the very structure of art and its recipient.

The sociological dimension

The shift towards a sociologically influenced aesthetics of reception is perhaps most clearly marked in the discussion of artistic norms. According to Mukařovský, the sociological aspect cannot be separated from a consideration of a norm:

> The approach to the problem of the aesthetic norm through sociology is not only a possible approach, or simply an ancillary one, but is, together with the noetic aspect of the problem, a basic requirement for research, since it enables us to investigate in detail the dialectical contradiction between the variability and multiplicity of the aesthetic norm and its rights to constant validity.   (*Aesthetic Function*, p. 58)

While Ingarden defines his standards in accordance with the classical ideal and the Formalists conceived of norms in terms of a purely literary realm of forms, Mukařovský considers the social interaction and movement of norms to be of primary importance. Although he is closer to the Formalist position in his reliance on perceptibility and the disturbance of the habitual, he recognizes that social classes and extra-aesthetic social relations play an important role in establishing and altering norms. Unlike the Formalists, he does not restrict his attention to avant-garde or "lofty art," but observes instead the penetration of "lofty art" into various strata of society as well as the influence of folk art on the so-called avant-garde. In fact, two of Mukařovský's most important conclusions about artistic norms are that they are not static, eternal constructs and that the coexistence of several different and even conflicting norms is a commonplace occurrence. One could contend with some justification that Mukařovský's conception of a norm thus represents a historicizing of Ingarden's sclerotic classicism and a socializing of the hermetic notion of literariness (*literaturnost'*) from the Formalist tradition.

Mukařovský's orientation towards the role of the perceiver in constituting the aesthetic object has far-reaching implications for the entire gamut of traditional literary terms. The concept of intentionality is a case in point (*Structure*, pp. 89–128). Like Wimsatt and Beardsley in the New Critical movement, Mukařovský dismisses the relevance of the originator's state of mind; nor does he wish to consider the question of intentionality as a psychological problem involving the conscious and subconscious elements of the creative process. In keeping with his notion of the work of art as an autonomous sign, he first removes

the artwork from any goal-oriented activity. Since the originator must have some practical attitude towards the artwork –
whether this is seen as overcoming technical difficulties in
creation or simply as the aim to complete the work – he/she is
not in a position to comprehend intentionality. The perceiver,
however, because he/she remains unrestrained by goal-oriented
considerations, can view the artwork as an autonomous sign.
Only the perceiver, therefore, is able to imbue the work of art
with the semantic unity that is then identified with intentionality. Thus Mukařovský can arrive at the following paradoxical
observation: "It is not the originator's attitude toward the work
but the perceiver's which is fundamental, or 'unmarked,' for
understanding its intrinsic artistic intent" (*Structure*, p. 97).
Only when the author or producer assumes the role of perceiver, i.e. only when he/she does not view the artwork as a task
to be completed or as a product, can he/she grasp intentionality.

Mukařovský's contribution to a reception-oriented problematic also extended into the area of what we would now call
the sociology of art. The establishing of artistic norms, the
evaluation of works of art, and the very function of art in a given
society cannot be separated from the conditions under which art
is produced, the possibilities for distribution, and a whole array
of factors relating to market conditions. By 1934 Mukařovský
recognized the importance of such considerations, as his objections to Shklovskii's position on literary sociology clearly
demonstrate (*Word*, pp. 134–42). In making an analogy between the literary text and the woven textile, Shklovskii had
written of his interest in examining only the "kinds of yarn" and
the "methods of weaving," not "the situation on the world
cotton market" (*Structure*, p. 140). Mukařovský, while not re-
gressing to the older biographical or vulgar sociological
"milieu" approaches to literature, contradicts Shklovskii from a
structuralist perspective. Literature according to him belongs
to a sphere of social phenomena composed of many series or
structures. Although one may affirm the *relative* autonomy of
any given series, no series is completely independent. The
"situation on the cotton market," in other words, by virtue of its
connection with the final fabric, is germane to the topic of
weaving. Thus the role of patronage, the book market, pub-

lishing houses, museums, or book clubs is a valid concern of literary investigation.

Vodička's contribution

Mukařovský's involvement with problems of literary reception is therefore a multifaceted affair. It was left to his student, Felix Vodička, however, to recognize reception theory in a more systematic fashion as a legitimate area for study. Whereas Mukařovský's dealings with aspects of reception are strewn throughout his work, and while he consequently never addresses the question of reception as a unified field for research, Vodička, in his outline of three fundamental tasks of literary history, includes reception-related problems in his third complex of issues.[3] He thus formalizes certain problematics that Mukařovský had dealt with in a variety of contexts.

Vodička's own contribution to reception theory involves his endeavor to reconcile Ingarden's phenomenological approach with his teacher's structuralist model.[4] Adopting Ingarden's concept of concretization, he attempts to overcome its ahistorical limitations by rejecting the notion of an ideal concretion and by connecting the term to the development of the aesthetic norm. Furthermore, Vodička expands the domain of the concept. While Ingarden stresses the concretization of the schematized aspects, he insists that the structure of the entire work takes on a new character when the circumstances involving time, place, or social conditions are altered. This concept of concretization is thus better equipped to cope with empirically observed differences in taste or with changes in the popularity of individual texts or in entire canons.

His preoccupation with actual literary history turns to his disadvantage, though, when he introduces the critic as the arbiter of adequate concretions. According to Vodička, the critic's function is to fix the concretion of literary works, to integrate them into the system of literary values. With this model of the critic one could argue that he has merely replaced Ingarden's ideal norm of adequate concretion with an ideal figure who formulates the concretion for given eras. The difference between the two theories consists only in Vodička's admission of a potential variety of responses. What is lost in both cases is the sociological situating of work and recipient that was the most attractive part of Mukařovský's semiological model.

Hans-Georg Gadamer

Hermeneutics and methodology

There is perhaps no contemporary theorist more concerned with the situated nature of our interpretations than Hans-Georg Gadamer, and doubtless his popularity in recent years is in no small part attributable to his radical insistence on the historical nature of understanding. That his work has been influential in the development of reception theory, however, is somewhat of an irony. For in his *magnum opus, Truth and Method* (1960),[1] Gadamer had sought to discredit precisely what many reception theorists seem to want most: a method, not only for studying and analyzing literature, but for arriving at the truth about the text. The "and" in Gadamer's title, in other words, should not be read in its conjunctive, but in its disjunctive sense. Although the main target in the book in this regard is the experimental method of the natural sciences, Gadamer's attack on method is certainly applicable to much of what has gone under the rubric of reception theory as well.

Method, for Gadamer, is something that a subject applies to an object to yield a specified result. In the case of the natural sciences, this result has been – erroneously, according to Gadamer – associated with truth. Gadamer's refurbishing of hermeneutics, the science of understanding and interpretation, is meant to counter this pernicious association. Against modern science's tendency "to absorb hermeneutical reflection into itself and render it serviceable to science,"[2] Gadamer proposes hermeneutics as a corrective and metacritical orientation to overcome the limitations of all methodological endeavor. Whereas hermeneutics had previously been involved with exegesis, the psychology of understanding (Friedrich Schleiermacher), or methodology in the human sciences (*Geisteswissenschaften*) (Wilhelm Dilthey), Gadamer claims for hermeneutics a universal status. He is interested in explaining understanding (*Verstehen*) as such, not in its relation to a particular discipline, but conceived as the essence of our being-in-the-world. In this sense his work is best viewed as an attempt to mediate between philosophy and science by going beyond "the restricted horizon of interest of scientific, theoretical methodology."[3]

The hegemony of science

Gadamer's concerns are thus philosophical and ontological in nature; *Truth and Method* introduces hermeneutics not to provide a new and better method, but to question methodology and its relationship to truth. To make this renovated task of hermeneutics more plausible, Gadamer imbeds two philosophical narratives in his book. The first, heavily indebted to Martin Heidegger, tells the story of the western philosophical tradition in the form of a fall from grace and the possibility of future redemption. In some pre-Cartesian time — particular reference is made to ancient Greece — the scientific method had not yet come to dominate the notion of truth. Subject and object, being and thinking, were not radically severed from one another as they became later. But with the advent of Cartesian dualism the alienation of western human beings, which had presumably been detectable long before Descartes, became the corner-stone of western philosophy. The unstated task of speculative activity from the seventeenth to the twentieth century has been to conceal and justify the alienation of mind and matter, subject and object, by providing a philosophical basis for the scientific method. "Scientific activity," Gadamer writes, "always has something Cartesian about it. It is the result of a critical method that seeks only to allow what cannot be doubted" (p. 211). In this scheme of philosophy Kant supplies the final epistemological apology for the natural sciences with his *Critique of Pure Reason* (1781).

> Kant had concluded the work on the problem of knowledge as it was posed by the emergence of the new science in the seventeenth century. The mathematico-scientific construction, of which the new sciences made use, was provided by Kant with the epistemological justification which it needed because its ideas had no other claims to existence than those of *entia rationis*.   (p. 194)

To highlight the hegemony of the natural scientific method, Gadamer devotes the first section of his book to a critique of aesthetic consciousness. The exclusion of art from truth and the reduction of the aesthetic sphere to a realm of mere appearance (*Schein*) as well as the various endeavors to associate or reassociate art and truth are the result of the "domination of the scientific epistemological model," which discredits "all the possibilities of knowing that lie outside this new method" (p. 75). Art thus constitutes a sphere that suffers a marked devaluation in the face of the privileged method; but it is also an area in which the deficiencies of that method are strikingly apparent. Art, therefore, is precisely the realm of philosophy that interests Gadamer most. For ultimately he is concerned with disclosing the opposition to the scientific method and with narrating the tale of the breakdown of the tyranny of this method, as the following comment indicates:

> Modern science has never entirely denied its Greek origin, however much, since the seventeenth century, it has become conscious of itself, and of the boundless possibilities that open up before it. Descartes' real treatise on method, his "Rules", the veritable manifesto of modern science, did not appear, as we know, until a long time after his death. However, his thoughtful meditations on the compatibility of the mathematical knowledge of nature with metaphysics set a task for an entire age. German philosophy from Leibniz to Hegel has constantly tried to supplement the new science of physics by a philosophical and speculative science in which the legacy of Aristotle would be revived and preserved. We need only recall Goethe's objection to Newton, which was shared by Schelling, Hegel and Schopenhauer.   (p. 417)

The completion of this first narrative therefore involves both the return to the traditional questions, such as those ontological problems Heidegger raises at the opening of *Being and Time* (1927),[4] and an examination of the traces of resistance to modern science's perversion of these questions. Both Heidegger and Gadamer, as revivers of the concern with universal understanding, are accordingly cast in the role of the most important authors of the final chapters of this philosophical story.

The history of hermeneutics

The second tale that Gadamer narrates, the history of hermeneutics, has similar concluding chapters, but a slightly
different plot, since hermeneutics is generally associated by
Gadamer with an opposition to the dominant scientific mode of
thought. It has a connection with art, too, in that Gadamer sees
the example of art as paradigmatic for the notion of understanding in general (pp. 146–50). But the beginning of this story
lies in the pre-Romantic era with the tradition of biblical
exegesis and humanistic endeavor. For Gadamer the origins of
hermeneutics are intimately linked with the concern to discover
the correct sense of texts. Hermeneutics, he writes, "claims to
reveal, by special techniques, the original meaning of the texts
in both traditions, humanistic literature and the Bible" (p.
154). If the activity of legal interpretation is added to these two
traditions, then we can see why pre-Romantic hermeneutics is
presented in terms of a threefold power: *subtilitas intelligendi*
(understanding), *subtilitas explicandi* (explication), and *subtilitas
applicandi* (application).

Once again this narrative is concerned with the loss of an
original state of existence. For hermeneutics in the course of its
rather uneven development forgets its threefold power and is
stripped eventually of its explanatory and applicative functions.
Gadamer relates in detail how the most important theoreticians
of the nineteenth and twentieth centuries tried to deal with the
problem of human understanding. In his discussions of Friedrich Schleiermacher, Leopold von Ranke, Friedrich Droysen,
and Wilhelm Dilthey, he points to their seminal contributions
to hermeneutical theory. But he also demonstrates how each in
his own way is unable to extricate himself from "methodological" thinking. At some point each of these writers has illicit
recourse to objectivity and objective knowledge, thus retaining
the pernicious subject–object duality inherent in the scientific
method.

The resolution of the hermeneutical dilemma, like the resus-
citation of western philosophy, involves Heidegger's overcoming of one final metaphysical obstacle, Edmund Husserl's
phenomenology. Husserl, of course, also regarded his philosophy as opposed both to objectivism and to metaphysics. But
his critique of the objectivism of all earlier philosophies was,

according to Gadamer, really "a methodological continuation of modern tendencies." Heidegger's project, by contrast, was conceived as "a return to the beginnings of western philosophy and the revival of the long-forgotten Greek argument about 'being'" (p. 227).

Heidegger's thesis in *Being and Time*, as Gadamer restates it in abbreviated and simplified form, is that "being itself is time" (p. 228). In contrast to Husserl, who postulated a transcendental, atemporal subject or proto-I, Heidegger situates all being in the world. Thus the life-world (*Lebenswelt*) could no longer be ignored or "bracketed" as Husserl demanded. Instead it must be considered the very essence of being. Finitude and temporality must stand at the center of the philosophical enterprise.

The ramifications of Heidegger's reformulation of philosophical enquiry for hermeneutics are enormous. Whereas, for science and the scientific method, historicity (i.e. the quality of being historical, finite, and temporal) had been an obstacle to the ideal of objective knowledge, it was now transformed into the very factor that enables understanding.

> The concept of understanding is no longer a methodological concept, as with Droysen. Nor, as in Dilthey's attempt to provide a hermeneutical ground for the human sciences, is the process of understanding an inverse operation that simply follows behind life's tendency towards ideality. Understanding is the original character of the being of human life itself.   (p. 230)

By rethinking the question of being, Heidegger thus destroys science's exclusive claim to truth and refocuses the project of hermeneutics on the always historical nature of understanding.

Hermeneutical prejudice

Gadamer understands his contribution to hermeneutics as a continuation of Heidegger's rethinking of being. Especially important for him is his predecessor's affirmation of the pre-structured nature of understanding. While previous theory had advocated a purging of preconceptions, Heidegger claims that it is precisely our being-in-the-world with its prejudices and presuppositions that makes understanding possible. As he writes in *Being and Time*: "Whenever something is interpreted as something, the interpretation will be founded essentially upon fore-having [*Vorhabe*], fore-sight [*Vorsicht*], and fore-conception [*Vorgriff*]. An interpretation is never a presuppositionless apprehending of something presented to us" (pp. 191–2). Or, in a slight rephrasing of this thought: "Meaning is the 'upon-which' [*Woraufhin*] of a projection in terms of which something becomes intelligible as something; it gets its structure from a fore-having, a fore-sight, and a fore-conception" (p. 193).

Gadamer takes up this issue most thoroughly in his discussion of prejudice (*Vorurteil*). The word in German, like its English equivalent, although etymologically related to pre-judging or merely forming a judgment about something beforehand, has come to mean a negative bias or a quality that excludes accurate judgment. The enlightenment, Gadamer claims, is responsible for this discrediting of the notion of prejudice. But this discrediting, he continues, is itself the result of a prejudice that is linked to the methodological claims to truth proposed by the natural sciences. Prejudice, because it belongs to historical reality itself, is not a hindrance to understanding, but rather a condition of the possibility of understanding. "What is necessary is a fundamental rehabilitation of the concept of prejudice and a recognition of the fact that there are legitimate prejudices, if we want to do justice to man's finite, historical mode of being" (p. 246).

Effective-history and the horizon of understanding

Gadamer's reliance on "prejudice" as a positive value may be seen, on the one hand, as a device for shocking liberal readers. But the serious point behind the rehabilitation of this notion should not go unnoticed either. For Gadamer is simply stating here that one's "prejudices" and preconceptions are a fundamental part of any hermeneutic situation. Thus, in contrast to previous hermeneutical theory, the historicality of the interpreter is not a *barrier* to understanding. A truly hermeneutical thinking must "take account of its own historicality" (*die eigene Geschichtlichkeit mitdenken*) (p. 267). It is only a "proper hermeneutics" when it demonstrates "the effectivity [*Wirklichkeit*] of history within understanding itself." Gadamer calls this type of hermeneutics "effective-history" (*Wirkungsgeschichte*). Now Gadamer is quick to caution that he is not trying to promote research that would develop a new method to take factors of effect into consideration; he is not making a plea for "a new independent discipline ancillary to the human sciences." Rather, he seems to be calling for a new consciousness – "effective-historical consciousness" (*wirkungsgeschichtliches Bewusstsein*) – that would recognize what is already occurring when we encounter the past. Whether one approves of effective-history or not, it is, according to Gadamer, intimately intertwined with our understanding, and effective-historical consciousness simply makes us aware of this reality: "Effective-historical consciousness is primarily consciousness of the hermeneutical situation" (p. 268).

To clarify what the hermeneutical situation entails, Gadamer begins by saying "that it represents a standpoint that limits the possibility of vision." Then, borrowing and adapting a term from Husserl's phenomenology, he proceeds to introduce the central notion of "horizon" as "an essential part of the concept of situation" (p. 289). Horizon thus describes our situatedness in the world, but it should not be thought of in terms of a fixed or closed standpoint; rather, it is "something into which we move and which moves with us" (p. 271). It may also be defined with reference to the prejudices that we bring with us at any given time, since these represent a "horizon" over which we cannot see. The act of understanding is then described in one of Gadamer's most notorious metaphors as a fusion of one's own horizon with the historical horizon (*Horizontverschmelzung*).

Gadamer concedes of course that the very notion of a separate horizon for, say, a literary text is illusory; there is no line that separates past from present horizon.

> When our historical consciousness places itself within historical horizons, this does not entail passing into alien worlds unconnected in any way with our own, but together they constitute the one great horizon that moves from within and, beyond the frontiers of the present, embraces the historical depths of our self-consciousness. It is, in fact, a single horizon that embraces everything contained in historical consciousness. (p. 271)

Yet this illusion, this "projecting of the historical horizon," is a necessary "phase in the process of understanding"; it is immediately followed by historical consciousness recombining "what it has distinguished in order . . . to be one again with itself." The fusing of horizons, Gadamer maintains, actually takes place, but it means "that as the historical horizon is projected, it is simultaneously removed" (p. 273). In an almost Hegelian manner, it seems that understanding is historical consciousness becoming aware of itself.

Application

This activity of consciousness is connected with what is probably Gadamer's most original contribution to modern hermeneutics. Relying on legal hermeneutics for his paradigm, Gadamer insists that every interpretation is simultaneously an application (*Anwendung*). Restoring the *subtilitas applicandi* to hermeneutics, however, is not a mere gesture towards recapturing the original function of the interpretative enterprise. Rather, it is an affirmation and logical consequence of the principles developed in connection with the effective-historical consciousness. Understanding means application for the present:

> The truth is that there is always contained in historical understanding the idea that the tradition reaching us speaks into the present and must be understood in this mediation – indeed, as this mediation. Legal hermeneutics is, then, in reality no special case but is, on the contrary, fitted to restore the full scope of the hermeneutical problem and so to retrieve the former unity of hermeneutics, in which jurist and theologian meet the student of the humanities.   (p. 293)

The controversy around Gadamer's concept of application seems to be another case of a provocative wording leading to an unnecessary dispute. Application is not to be understood as praxis in the Marxist sense or as the performance of a physical deed. It does not entail a perceptible taking from the text and putting into activity in the real world. Rather, it is more akin to what Ingarden calls "concretion," an actualizing or making-present for the interpreter. In this sense a comparison could be drawn between a theater director interpreting a script and realizing it in performance, and the reader's activity in understanding a text. Both include application in Gadamer's sense. But we might also think of application within the frame of Gadamer's central analogy between the process of understanding and the dialogue. When we encounter a text, according to this model, we enter into a conversation with the past in which the give-and-take, the questioning and answering involved in an openness to the other, leads to understanding. Application, then, can be described as a "mediating between then and now, between the 'Thou' and the 'I'" (p. 298). Seen as concretion or mediation, the concept of application loses some of its original appeal, and Gadamer in his retrieval of the lost sense of hermeneutics is thus far less radical than he appears at first glance.

The classical bias

Despite Gadamer's methodological disclaimers, his philosophical hermeneutics has been fecund soil for reception theorists. His notions of effective-history and horizon have been the items most frequently appropriated, especially by Hans Robert Jauss and his students. Yet one cannot help feeling that Gadamer's impact has been the result of a misunderstanding. However useful the terms "horizon of expectations" (*Erwartungshorizont*) and effective-history have become for examining literary texts, they belong in Gadamer's theory to a more abstract, philosophical realm. And although one can claim that methodology is always implied in any notion of hermeneutics, Gadamer obviously does not agree.

Perhaps the central controversy in contemporary German hermeneutics has focused on the role of tradition in Gadamer's work. Most often theorists have objected to his reliance on the "classical" as exemplary for effective-history. Although the classical for Gadamer is simply what has been preserved because it has been found worthy of preserving, critics have justifiably charged that in utilizing such a notion Gadamer ignores the power relationships inherent in any socially mediated text or social exchange. Since language itself is not a neutral instrument, Gadamer's dialogical model, his ideal communication between past and present as conversation between two speakers, is both a distortion of what really occurs in understanding, and itself an ideological ploy serving to obfuscate the concrete social relations within which communication occurs.

Gadamer has not been at a loss for replies to his detractors, but his failure to integrate a social perspective into his general theoretical framework remains a weakness in his work. Like Heidegger, he seems able to admit historicality only on an abstract theoretical level. When he himself analyzes texts – whether it is a poem by Rilke or a novel by Karl Immermann – the potentially radical notion of being-in-the-world produces a philosophical criticism akin to the most ahistorical, New Critical readings.

Sociology of literature

Leo Löwenthal: psycho sociology

The social situating of literary texts that is missing in Gadamer's ontological hermeneutics appears to be a task for what has been called the sociology of literature. Before the Second World War in Germany this branch of literary study was not very well developed, so it should come as no surprise that sociologically oriented forerunners to reception theory were rare. Indeed, a leitmotif in the few essays or books that were written in this field is the plaint regarding the previous neglect of this area and the call for more research into literary effect and reception. In 1932, for example, Leo Löwenthal could still note the lack of interest in this aspect of critical endeavor; in fact, the very absence of research is for him an important sign of the state of literary scholarship:

> It is sociologically interesting that a task like the study of the effect of literary works, which is so important and central for research, has been almost entirely ignored, even though there exists in journals and newspapers, in letters and memoirs, an infinite amount of material that would teach us about the reception of literature in specific social groups and by individuals.[1]

Although Löwenthal emphasizes here the great amount of easily accessible information, he is not primarily interested in empirical research; for this would entail only a continuation of the "mere philology" and the "collection of data" to which reception studies should provide an alternative. Rather, what he advocates is a more thoroughgoing exploration of psycho-sociological characteristics within social structures. Indeed, psychology supplies the link that will make aesthetics possible as a discipline. "Without a psychology of art, without the study of the unconscious stimulants that are involved in the psychological triangle of writer, literature, and recipient, there is no poetic aesthetics." Freudian psychology becomes for Löwenthal an indispensable aid for dealing with the sociology of reception, for investigating "the problem of the relationship between work and recipient, a problem that until now has been repeatedly pushed into the background" (*Erzählkunst*, pp. 27–8).

Löwenthal's own contribution to a socio-psychological reception theory of literature is contained in his pioneering study of Dostoyevsky's reception in pre-First World War Germany.[2] By examining the various essays and books written on the Russian novelist, he is able to explain his appropriation and theoretical significance for particular groups in Wilhelmine Germany. Dostoyevsky, he demonstrates, served as an ideological crutch for members of the German middle classes, providing them with a series of myths that made sense to individuals caught between a powerful upper class and a rapidly rising proletariat. But more important than the conclusions of this one case study are the general theoretical statements that inform the investigation. Löwenthal insists on the very first page that the effect of a literary work belongs to its very being: "what it is, is determined essentially by the way it is experienced" (p. 343). Human experience, however, is itself largely preconditioned, and for this reason the analysis of the reception of an author's work involves an understanding of the "life process" of the society (p. 343). Literature, in turn, interfaces with society in a complex fashion. On the one hand, for specific social groups it fulfills psychological needs that would otherwise threaten the social order.

Art in general, according to Löwenthal, can contribute to

a satisfaction of the phantasy (*Phantasiebefriedigung*), and the internalization inherent in this process obviates real social gratification. The study of the reception and consumption of literature is therefore not only the investigation of an essential literary problem, but also a contribution to social analysis; for it entails an examination of "factors that, beyond the mere apparatus of power, exercise a socially conservative and retarding function through their psychic power" (p. 369).

On the other hand, it would be undialectical to reduce the function of art to its role in ideological and psychological pacification; intrinsic to art is resistance to society as well.

> Although it is true that in the total social process it [art] has the function of reconciliation with the existing order, it also encompasses an element of dissatisfaction that has to be reconciled. In its very fabric is contained in principle the resistance, the contradiction to the existing order. (pp. 380–1)

For Löwenthal, then, reception entails both a socially conditioned and a psychologically conditioning force; ideology as well as the resistance to ideology; both a gratification of needs and the displacement of gratification.

Julian Hirsch: reception and historiography

This socio-psychological method of dealing with the problem of reception not only produced an exemplary case study, but also contained several revolutionary implications for literary theory in general. But Löwenthal was primarily concerned with a specific instance (Dostoyevsky) at a particular time in German history (1880–1920); only the few remarks discussed above point to a framework that would encompass the question of reception as such. A theory of this nature, however, would not only have to include sociology and psychology, but also reflect upon basic problems of historiography. For, as Jauss and others have noted, the question of reception is intimately linked to the writing of history. Why a given work or author becomes famous, how that fame is perpetuated over periods of time, what factors increase or diminish a reputation – all of these questions involve the historian as much as the sociologist or psychologist.

Although these matters were occasionally the object of speculation by nineteenth-century historians – Droysen and Ranke are
only two examples – they received scant attention in Germany
in the early part of the twentieth century.

One of the notable exceptions in this regard was contained in
a book by Julian Hirsch entitled *Die Genesis des Ruhmes* (The
Genesis of Fame).[3] In this study, significantly subtitled "A
Contribution to the Methodology of History", Hirsch sets himself the task of examining how and why a judgment concerning
fame arises. This manner of posing the question is itself a radical
break from past practices, since the more usual questions
concern how eminent individuals arise and what effects these
persons have on their times and the future. The form of *these*
questions, however, suggests that there are objective answers,
that the eminence of the individual is itself an objective fact, and
that the individual therefore determines the effects, rather than
the conditions that give rise to the effects determining the very
eminence of the individual. What Hirsch does by asking the
question in this altered form is to switch the emphasis from the
object (the eminent individual) to the evaluating or perceiving
subject (the person or groups that attribute fame to the individual). In other words, instead of falling into the objectivist
snare, he asks the question from a reception-theoretical standpoint (pp. 9–10).

Hirsch's book thus examines those factors that constitute the
conditions under which an individual is judged to be famous.
Fame for Hirsch entails recognition by the masses, so that those
institutions contributing to a general recognition of "eminence"
are deemed most important. In modern times, schools, the
press, popular journals, as well as more traditional vehicles like
works of art, are some of the most common ways for establishing
and perpetuating fame (pp. 128–90). Indeed, not only are the
subject's views and opinions formed by these institutions. In
certain cases, even if a dissenting opinion were by some chance
formulated, it would be dismissed for its very difference from the
norm. In this connection Hirsch brings up the hypothetical
example of the training of a Shakespearean scholar. Having
been told from childhood that Shakespeare is the greatest
English writer and having later read in journals about
Shakespeare's genius and mastery of dramatic technique, this

student of English literature could hardly be expected to possess anything except an admiration for the English bard. To escape the influence of the vast tradition of enthusiasm for Shakespeare is almost impossible: "The power of social heredity already weighs so heavily on the future researcher that he can no longer escape it." If a negative appraisal were perchance offered, it would be treated by other experts as foolishness or as a sacrilege (pp. 250–1).

What Hirsch reveals with this capsule academic career is not only that the effect of a work or an individual is inseparable from its history of having an effect, or that social conditions predetermine our evaluations and, in turn, their impact. He also demonstrates that our judgments about past individuals are based on their phenomenological form, the way they appear to us rather than the way they are or were. For this reason he proposes that the study of biography be supplemented by what he calls *Phänographik* or the study of the individual as a phenomenon (pp. 270–8). The importance of such studies has hitherto gone unnoticed, according to Hirsch; if the essence of an individual's life includes his/her influence and fame, then the historian or biographer cannot do without "phenography." "Every individual, whether an artist or a person of action, who has in any way 'appeared' [*erscheint*], i.e. who has had any kind of mass effect, can only be perceived [*erkannt*] when the development of the phenomenal forms is presented" (p. 278). This demand for phenographics, which resembles so many of the statements by reception theorists, suggests a historiography in which historicism is replaced by what Gadamer calls, in his ontological context, effective-history. It would substitute for the objective depiction of events and individuals the history of their becoming events and individuals for us.

Levin Schücking: the sociology of taste

Suggestive as Hirsch's study is for literary history, it remained for the following generation without influence among literary scholars. Literary history for the most part was still considered in terms of the production and description of works, not their reception. One of the few alternatives to the dominant notions of literary history, however, was offered by Levin L. Schücking. In contrast to Hirsch, who concerned himself with the fame of individuals, Schücking postulated that the key to understanding literary history lay in an investigation of taste, one of the neglected areas of previous scholarship.

For Schücking, "taste" designates a general receptiveness for art, a "relationship to art in which a man's entire philosophy of life is mirrored or at any rate one where the inmost being of the man himself is involved."[4] It is not a constant quality or a universal organ, but rather something that alters over time, between cultures, and even inside societies. Related to the *Zeitgeist* or spirit of the age (pp. 1–9), it is responsible not only for the evaluation and, in some instances, canonization of works and authors, but also for the literature written at that time. The study of the history of taste or the formation of taste (*Geschmacks-bildung*) thus constitutes the primary task for the literary historian. As Schücking wrote in 1913: "What was read at a specific time in various strata of the nation and why it was read – this should be the chief question of literary history."[5] As we have observed before, this formulation of the problem entails a radical shift from the usual emphasis. The process of creation and the examination of the literary qualities of the work give way here to an exploration of the public, its preferences, and the reasons for reading habits. No longer do the author and his/her *œuvre* stand in the foreground, but rather the consumer and the conditions under which consumption occurs.

Accordingly Schücking envisions a wide variety of tasks for literary scholars who follow his lead. Like Hirsch, he emphasizes the importance of specific institutions that contribute to the taste of a given era. Forces that maintain taste, such as schools and universities, or organizations that seek to influence trends, such as literary clubs and libraries, as well as book stores and publishers, are recognized as essential elements of literary history (pp. 72–108). Schücking also devotes considerable attention to the factors that cause changes in taste. He points out that such disparate events as revolutions (p. 82), the introduction of coffee to Europe (p. 37), or the democratization of German society after the First World War (p. 37) have been responsible for differing attitudes towards art and literature.

Schücking's most important theoretical contribution, however, concerns the question of how we determine the dominant taste for a given period. To answer this question, he introduces the notion of a culture-bearing stratum (*kulturtragende Schicht*) in society made up of those who propagate taste (*Geschmacks-trägertypen*). Art is ultimately dependent on these propagators of taste, and "the ability of such groups to assert themselves is again dependent on the degree of power they can exercise within the social structure" (p. 89). Their power is determined primarily by the extent to which they dominate "the mechanism of artistic life" (p. 89). Schücking stresses that domination should not be understood exclusively in a material sense – the actual owning of a publishing house, for example – but that it is not completely non-material either. The relationship between ownership and ideas, he demonstrates, is a complex matter (pp. 78–92). What is ultimately important about this type of analysis is the recognition that even what is inherited by us as the taste of past eras, what Gadamer describes as "classic," is only the choice of a small group. What has been canonized are thus works selected by individuals in a position of power. Or, as Schücking phrases it at one point in his study, it is not the good that asserts itself through tradition; rather "that which wins through will thereafter be regarded as good" (p. 58). Although the specific connection remains undeveloped, this manner of approaching literary history places the power relationships in a society at the very center of aesthetic evaluation.

Impact in post-war Germany

Unfortunately, the implications for literary criticism in the works of Schücking, Hirsch, and Löwenthal went virtually unnoticed. Even after the Second World War, when German society supposedly sought a new beginning in literature and scholarship, there were few attempts made in the west to examine literary history from the standpoint of the sociology of literature. During the 1960s, however, as younger scholars began to seek alternatives to the superannuated methods of their older colleagues, a revival of sociological concern took place. Much of the resulting scholarship focused on traditional problems of authors and works; but some emphasis was also placed on the book market, the public, and the sociology of readers.

It is probably not fortuitous that the boom in sociological studies occurs at about the same time that the first manifestos of reception theory appear. For reception theorists, although they often did not draw directly from the pre-war sociology of literature or from the flood of sociologically based studies of the 1960s, were occupied with some of the same issues that appear in sociological research, especially when the topic entailed the connection between literature and the public. The relationship of the sociology of literature to reception theory, then, is probably not one of direct impact or simple cause and effect. But the increasing concern for sociological investigations almost certainly contributed to the atmosphere in which reception theory became possible and prospered.

3

The major theorists

From the history of reception to aesthetic experience: Hans Robert Jauss

Literary history and historiography

In contrast to the "precursors" to reception theory, whose preoccupations were primarily philosophical, psychological, or sociological, Hans Robert Jauss's interest in matters of reception originates in his concern with the relationship between literature and history. In his earlier theoretical work in particular he concentrates most often on the disrepute into which literary history has fallen and possible remedies for this situation. What he detects in German and international scholarship of the 1960s is a growing disregard for the historical nature of literature, as scholars and critics turned to a variety of sociological psychoanalytical, semasiological, *gestalt*-psychological, or aesthetically oriented methods.[1] His stated goal is to help to restore history to the center of literary studies, and it is in this context that the two titles of his "manifesto" of reception theory should be understood.

When delivered at Constance in April 1967 as an inaugural address, the now notorious lecture contained clear allusions to Friedrich Schiller's initial speech as a historian at Jena in 1789. The title Jauss chose, "What is and for what purpose does one study literary history?" – which modifies Schiller's title only by the insertion of "literary" for "universal" – is meant to evoke his illustrious predecessor in at least two ways. First, it establishes a sense of urgency in a field that seemed moribund and consequently in need of a new orientation. Jauss's attitude toward the contemporary study of literature, outlined in his "Paradigm" essay as well as in other works of the period, is that the rationale for a continued occupation with literature is lacking, especially in view of the demise of older models of interpretation. That Schiller's talk was delivered just prior to the outbreak of the French Revolution must certainly have occurred to Jauss when he selected his title. The intent is to shock, to announce a "revolution" in the making, to proclaim the end of the *ancien régime* of literary scholarship.

What is needed to revive the study of literature – and this is the second connection with Schiller's lecture – is to restore some vital link between the artefacts of the past and the concerns of the present, as Schiller had advocated 178 years before. For literary scholarship and instruction such a connection can be established only if literary history is no longer relegated to the periphery of the discipline, Jauss maintains. Hence the revised title of his lecture, "Literary history as a provocation for literary scholarship," stresses the active side of his endeavors.[2] To make the study of literature relevant once again, the establishment needs to be challenged by this quasi-Schillerian call-to-arms.

It is important to remember, however, that Jauss's essay is a provocation, not a plea for a revival. The allusions to Schiller and the express intent to restore the integrity and centrality of literary history should not be read as a conservative or reactionary critical maneuver. Indeed, it is the very obsolescence of the older notions of literary historiography, according to Jauss, that have produced the current predicament. The German idealist conception of history, the major paradigm for Schiller's era, had recourse to a telos or guiding principle for the ordering of events and facts.

The most notable literary history in this tradition was Georg Gottfried Gervinus's *History of the Poetic National Literature of the Germans* (1835–42). In accord with most nineteenth-century historians, Gervinus's guiding idea was connected with his sense of national identity – in contrast, it should be noted, to the more cosmopolitan goals of freedom or humanity posited by earlier universal histories. The problem with this variety of historiography became evident with the questioning of the teleological model. The historian was faced with the dilemma of either projecting a closure into some future time and reading events backwards from this hypothetical point, or considering the goal as already achieved, thereby implying that subsequent events were either inconsequential or part of a general demise. When Gervinus narrated a culmination of German literary history in classicism, he chose the latter alternative, although his intent was certainly to foster and project the national unity that Germany had not yet achieved.

As Jauss points out, the major alternative to this teleologically based historiography arose with historicism in the nineteenth century. The most noted proponent of this school, Leopold von Ranke, propagated the notion of full objectivity – and total relativity – with the following notorious utterance: "But I maintain that each period is immediate *vis-à-vis* God, and that its value depends not at all on what followed from it, but rather on its own existence, on its own self'" (p. 7). But the postulate of the dignity and self-sufficiency of every era is maintained only at the price of annihilating the link between past and present that Schiller – and in his footsteps Jauss – so passionately defends. In its zeal to avoid speculation on final ends, historicism sacrifices the relevance of history to a dubious ideal of objectivity.

The results for literary studies are, according to Jauss's presentation, twofold. On the one hand we find the appearance of literary methodologies that, in response to this crisis of historiography, adopt principles that make the writing of literary history problematic. In aping the methods of the natural sciences, positivism treated literary works as if they were the consequences of verifiable and measurable causes:

> The application of the principle of pure causal explanation to the history of literature brought only externally determining factors to light, allowed source study to grow to a hyper-trophied degree, and dissolved the specific character of the literary work into a collection of "influences" that could be increased at will.   (p. 8)

But the reaction to literary positivism in Germany, *Geistesge-schichte* (literally: the history of the spirit; but similar to the history of ideas), was equally unable to reconcile literature and history. "Geistesgeschichte took hold of literature, opposed the causal explanation of history with an aesthetics of irrational creation, and sought the coherence of literature [*Dichtung*] in the recurrence of atemporal ideas and motifs" (p. 8).

On the other hand, the actual literary histories written under the aegis of such methodologies have rightly been criticized for their theoretical inadequacies. In order to avoid a banal chronicle of dates and works, the prospective literary historian was presented with two alternatives. The first proposes organizing the literary canon around general tendencies, genres, and other such categories, thus enabling the subsumption of individual works chronologically under these headings. The other popular method deals with only major authors in blocks; thus this type of literary history would frequently consist of a series of abbreviated "life-and-works" essays. Neither solution is satisfactory: the former most often winds up being a history of culture with literary examples, while the latter is really a collection of essays bound together by the coincidence of loose chronological ties and nationality. Moreover, Jauss notes, both of these traditional varieties of literary history are unable to come to terms with questions of evaluation. Oriented on the questionable ideal of objectivity propagated by historicist and positivist methodologies, these histories practice an "aesthetic abstinence" (p. 5) that abjures judgments of quality.

Looking at the problem of literary historiography in another way, as one of bringing together history and aesthetics, we might with Jauss put the question in terms of the two adversary methodologies of Marxism and Formalism. Marxism, as we have seen before, represents for Jauss an outmoded literary practice belonging to an essentially historicist-positivist paradigm. In his "Provocation" essay Jauss singles out the concept of "reflection" (*Widerspiegelung*) as particularly regressive and idealist, criticizing Georg Lukács and Lucien Goldmann – somewhat unfairly – for viewing literature only as the passive mirror of the external world. Yet despite Jauss's repudiation of most earlier Marxist theory, he recognizes both in the insistence on the historicity of literature and in some theoretical remarks by less conventional critics like Werner Krauss, Roger Garaudy, and Karel Kosík, that Marxism is not a monolithic, dogmatic system. Most important for him in this regard are the utterances that indicate a sensitivity toward issues of effect and reception.

The Formalists, on the other hand, are credited by Jauss with introducing aesthetic perception as a theoretical tool for exploring literary works. The shortcoming of the Formalist method in Jauss's view has to do with, first of all, the tendency towards a *l'art-pour-l'art* aesthetic. In Formalist theory

> the process of perception in art appears as an end in itself, the "tangibility of form" as its specific characteristic, and the "discovery of the device" [*Verfahren*] as the principle of a theory. This theory made art criticism into a rational method in conscious renunciation of historical knowledge, and thereby brought forth critical achievements of lasting scholarly value. (pp. 16–17)

In fact, even when Formalists like Tynianov or Eikhenbaum ventured into the area of literary historiography, they tended to restrict their views to the literary. Although they succeeded in elucidating a concept of evolution as it applies to the literary series, they were unable to connect this literary evolution with more general historical developments. The task for a new literary history, therefore, becomes to merge successfully the best qualities of Marxism and Formalism. This can be accomplished by satisfying the Marxist demand for historical mediations while retaining the Formalist advances in the realm of aesthetic perception.

The "aesthetics of reception"

Jauss's attempt to overcome the Marxist–Formalist dichotomy involves viewing literature from the perspective of the reader or consumer. The "aesthetics of reception" (*Rezeptionsästhetik*), as Jauss called his theory in the late 1960s and early 1970s, maintains that the historical essence of an artwork cannot be elucidated by examining its production or by simply describing it. Rather, literature should be treated as a dialectical process of production *and reception*. "Literature and art only obtain a history that has the character of a process when the succession of works is mediated not only through the producing subject, but also through the consuming subject – through the interaction of author and public" (p. 15). Jauss seeks to meet the Marxist demand for historical mediations by situating literature in the larger process of events; he retains the Formalist achievements by placing the perceiving subject at the center of his concerns. Thus history and aesthetics are united:

> The aesthetic implication lies in the fact that the first reception of a work by the reader includes a test of its aesthetic value in comparison with works already read. The obvious historical implication of this is that the understanding of the first reader will be sustained and enriched in a chain of receptions from generation to generation; in this way the historical significance of a work will be decided and its aesthetic value made evident.   (p. 20)

This shift in attention thus has implications for a new type of literary history as well. What Jauss envisions is a historiography that will play a conscious, mediating role between past and present. Instead of simply accepting the tradition as a given, the historian of literary reception will be called upon to rethink constantly the works in the canon in light of how they have affected and are affected by current conditions and events.

> The step from the history of the reception of the individual work to the history of literature has to lead to seeing and representing the historical consequence of works as they determine and clarify the coherence of literature, to the extent that it is meaningful, for us, as the prehistory of its present experience.   (p. 20)

With this sort of practice, literature becomes meaningful as a source of mediation between past and present, while literary history, in keeping with Jauss's Schillerian ideal, becomes central for literary studies because it enables us to comprehend past meanings as part of present practices.

The "horizon of expectations"

The integration of history and aesthetics, Marxism and Formalism, is accomplished largely by the introduction of the notion of a "horizon of expectations" (*Erwartungshorizont*), by Jauss's own

account the "methodological centerpiece" of his most important theoretical essay.[3] The term "horizon," as we have seen
above, was quite familiar in German philosophical circles.
Gadamer, we will recall, had used it to refer to "the range of
vision that includes everything that can be seen from a particular vantage point."[4] In similar contexts his predecessors Husserl and Heidegger had likewise introduced this notion. The
compound usage with "expectations" was not completely novel
either. Both the philosopher of science Karl Popper and the
sociologist Karl Mannheim had adopted the term long before
Jauss. It even had a previous association with cultural affairs.
In *Art and Illusion* the art historian E. H. Gombrich, under
Popper's influence, had defined the "horizon of expectation" as
a "mental set, which registers deviation and modifications with
exaggerated sensitivity."[5] Thus "horizon" and "horizon of
expectations" occur in a wide range of contexts, from German
phenomenological theory to the history of art.

The trouble with Jauss's use of the term "horizon" is that it is
so vaguely defined that it could include or exclude any previous
sense of the word. In fact, nowhere does he delineate precisely
what he means by it. When he discusses its origins late in his
"Provocation" essay, he cites his earlier references to the term
in 1959 and 1961; but turning to these writings we find a similar
lack of specificity.[6] Furthermore, the term is found in a variety of
compound words or phrases. Jauss refers to a "horizon of
experience," a "horizon of experience of life," a "horizon
structure," a "horizonal change," and a "material horizon of
conditions" (*materieller Bedingungshorizont*). The relationship
among these various uses is left just as nebulous as the category
"horizon" itself. Jauss seems to bank on the reader's common
sense in understanding at least his main term. "Horizon of
expectations" would appear to refer to an intersubjective system or structure of expectations, a "system of references" or a
mind-set that a hypothetical individual might bring to any text.

Such a provisional definition, however, does not alleviate the
central difficulties in usage. For example, one of Jauss's important methodological postulates concerns the "objectification" of
this horizon. The "ideal case" for an objectification involves
works that parody or reflect upon the literary tradition; *Don
Quixote*, *Jacques le Fataliste*, and *Chimères* are the illustrations

mentioned by name, although Shklovskii's "typical" novel, *Tristram Shandy*, would have no trouble fitting into this group as well. These works are ideal because they "evoke the reader's horizon of expectations, formed by a convention of genre, style, or form, only in order to destroy it step by step" (p. 24). Here the literary horizon is objectified because the work itself makes it an object perceivable by the reader. For works that are less directly evocative of expectations, Jauss suggests three general approaches to constructing the horizon:

> First, through familiar norms or the immanent poetics of the genre; second, through the implicit relationships to familiar works of the literary-historical surroundings; and third, through the opposition between fiction and reality, between the poetic and the practical function of language, which is always available to the reflective reader during the reading as a possibility of comparison. (p. 24)

The problem here is not so much the procedure that Jauss proposes, which is more or less what many literary scholars do when they relate a work to the literary tradition and the social structure, but rather the notion of objectification itself. Although Jauss at times endeavors to retain the transcendental nature of the horizon, by positing its objectifiability, he suggests an empirical procedure. Moreover, the method he indicates for objectifying the category presupposes a neutral position from which these observations can be made. The "familar standards" for a given era are verifiable only by assuming that from a present perspective we can make objective judgments of what these standards actually were. In contradistinction to Gadamer's insistence on historicality, we are asked here to ignore or bracket our own historical situatedness. Despite his struggle to escape a positivist-historicist paradigm, then, Jauss, in adopting objectivity as a methodological principle, appears to fall back into the very errors he criticizes.

Analogous difficulties arise when he tries to explain how his horizon of expectations avoids "the threatening pitfalls of psychology" (p. 22) and the "circular recourse to a general 'spirit of the age'" (p. 28), two of the strongest selling points for the concept. In the first instance Jauss is attempting to overcome the limitations of I. A. Richards's psychologically based aesthetics of response. He cites with approval René Wellek's criticism of Richards regarding the insufficiency of this approach for examining the meaning of the work of art and the consequent reduction of such a method to, at best, a sociology of taste. To counter this reduced version of reception and to go beyond individual responses, Jauss turns to textual linguistics:

> The psychic process in the reception of a text is, in the primary horizon of aesthetic experience, by no means only an arbitrary series of merely subjective impressions, but rather the carrying out of specific instructions in a process of directed perception, which can be comprehended according to its constitutive motivations and triggering signals, and which also can be described by a textual linguistics   (p. 23)

Relying on the work of Wolf-Dieter Stempel, he redefines the process of reception in terms of "the expansion of a semiotic system that is carried out between the development and the correction of a system" (p. 23). In this scheme the examination of the "process of the continuous establishing and altering of horizons" by means of textual and generic clues would elim-inate the individual variability of response, and, at least in theory, we could then establish a "transsubjective horizon of understanding" that determines "the influence of the text" (p. 23).

The problem here is that Jauss is still operating – apparently against his hermeneutical intentions – with an objectivist model. Signals appear as signals only within a certain mode or framework of perception. Genres, as conventional categories for dividing up the pie of literary works, are "facts" only because we or the author of a poetics has claimed that certain features of works merit grouping them together. Again, this is not to say that proceeding in this fashion is wrong or uncommon; the objection here is that Jauss is theorizing at cross purposes with his express intentions. He avoids psychology only by reintro-ducing an objectivist moment at odds with his hermeneutical premises. For this reason he, too, must have recourse to the vicious circle he ascribes to *Geistesgeschichte*. As long as he insists on the possibility of a "reconstruction of the horizon of expecta-tions" (p. 28) and sets out to accomplish this reconstruction with evidence or signals from the works themselves, he is going to be measuring the effect or impact of works against a horizon that is abstracted from those works.

This circle that Jauss does not quite manage to escape has consequences for his remarks on aesthetic value as well, since the contrast between a given work and the horizon stands at the heart of his theory of evaluation. Drawing heavily on the writings of the Russian Formalists, Jauss contends that the artistic character of a work can be determined "by the kind and the degree of its influence on a presupposed audience." Aesthetic distance, defined as the difference or separation between the horizon of expectations and the work or as the "change of horizons" (*Horizontwandel*), can be measured by the "spectrum of the audience's reaction and criticism's judgments" (p. 25).

This mechanistic approach to evaluation leads Jauss into a number of predicaments. Not the least of these is how to stipulate when a work has disappointed, or exceeded, or destroyed expectations. Even if one could find a measure for "disappointment," one would have to supplement this hypothesis of "value as difference" with a notion of "likeness that permits recognition." If the random typing of a chimpanzee was published as a novel, for example, it would certainly distance itself from the expectations of the reading public. But for a contemporary audience or any critic even to deal with this piece of "literature" as a serious endeavor, it would have to conform more closely to some recognizable literary norms. The distance between horizon and work, in other words, is an inadequate criterion for determining literary value.

This one-sidedness in Jauss's early theory is also responsible for the proximity in which he is forced to bring "culinary" or pulp literature and the classics. Both categories of literature, because they form a background of normal expectations, should manifest no "artistic character." As Jauss himself concedes, "their [the so-called masterpieces'] beautiful form that has become self-evident, and their seemingly unquestionable 'eternal meaning' bring them, according to an aesthetics of reception, dangerously close to the irresistibly convincing and enjoyable 'culinary' art" (pp. 25–6). But if special effort is needed to read the masterpieces "against the grain" in order that their greatness be recognized, one might legitimately ask why this type of reading is not also available for pulp literature. And if it is not – which one must assume would be Jauss's position – what other features then constitute the "artistic character" of the work?

The root of the problem lies in the almost exclusive reliance on the Formalists' theory of perception through defamiliarization (*ostranenie*) to establish value. Novelty apparently serves here as the sole criterion for evaluation, and although Jauss makes an attempt at one point to consider "the new" (*das Neue*) as a historical as well as an aesthetic category, he too often universalizes its function in determining aesthetic value. This orientation towards innovation is peculiar in the light of Jauss's extensive work in medieval literature. While most of the Formalists were influenced by current literary practices that stressed the destruction of conventions, many past eras, as Jauss surely knows, appear to have appreciated works as much for their similarity with, as their difference from, traditional norms. During medieval times, for example, the demand in artistic production was focused more on repeating certain structures than on breaking them. Although we may in retrospect value works that differed from the norm, it is doubtful that this type of judgment has been adhered to for very long.

The emphasis on novelty seems to be part of a modern prejudice, probably related to the penetration of market mechanisms into the aesthetic realm. Originality and genius were latecomers to the roster of favored evaluative categories, and it is quite possible that the sweeping change in the system of production – from feudalism, with its emphasis on hierarchy, regularity, and repetition, to capitalism with its ideology of ingenuity and its demand for constantly revolutionizing production – played a large part in the creation and reception of art as well. Our bias for something new or unique, in other words, most likely has much more to do with our own "horizon" than the thought or expectations that existed in past eras.

Towards a new literary history

Jauss relies heavily on Russian Formalism in one other important area. In sketching his considerations for the writing of a new sort of literary history, he adopts the Formalist notion of a diachronous literary series. There are three features of the Formalist discussion that are especially attractive for him. The first is that, in a literary history utilizing principles of the evolutionary series, the possibilities are maximized for linking aesthetic categories that, in traditional histories, are rarely associated by anything more than a general chronology. Second, a Formalist history would eliminate the teleological control on which most previous literary histories have depended. Instead of reading events backwards from a hypothetical end point, the evolutionary method postulates a *"dialectical self-production of new forms"* (p. 33). This method has the additional advantage of simplifying the criteria for selection of works:

> The criterion here is the work as a new form in the literary series, and not the self-reproduction of worn-out forms, artistic devices, and genres, which pass into the background until at a new moment in the evolution they are made "perceptible" once again.   (p. 33)

Finally, because novelty has been posited as both an aesthetic and a historical criterion, the Formalist literary history combines artistic and historical significance, thus reconciling the antagonism with which Jauss is most concerned. The advance in this final area may, of course, be illusory, since to overcome the separation of the historical and the aesthetic, the former has simply been defined in terms of the latter. Jauss's own dissatisfaction with a Formalist literary history, however, touches upon a different issue. For him the mere description of a change in structures, devices, or forms is not sufficient to delineate the function of a given work within the historical series:

> To determine this [function], that is, to recognize the problem left behind to which the new work in the historical series is the answer, the interpreter must bring his own experience into play, since the past horizon of old and new forms, problems and solutions, is only recognizable in its further mediation within the present horizon of the received work.   (p. 34)

This consideration may serve well for explaining how we understand a text but, as a basis for historiography, it is not very practical. By introducing the subjective and vague criterion of experience (*Erfahrung*), Jauss has in effect built immediate obsolescence into the writing of literary history. Since the past is only recognizable "in its further mediation within the present horizon," and since the present horizon is presumably changing constantly, it is difficult to understand how the modified dia-chronic model could be a foundation for anything but the most ephemeral of literary histories. None the less, this perspective does mark a noticeable change from earlier postulates concerning the necessity to objectify past horizons. For here Jauss calls upon the experience, not the neutrality, of the interpreter, defining the writing of literary history in a Gadamerian fashion as the "fusion of horizons" rather than the objectivistic descrip-tion of their succession in time.

The diachrony that Jauss adapts from the evolutionary model would be complemented in his new version of literary history by synchronic aspects. In this regard he proposes that literary historians examine selected "cross-sections" of liter-ary life in order to ascertain which works at any particular time stand out from the horizon and which works remain undis-tinguished. With this procedure one could produce various structures that are operative at a given historical moment, and by comparing one synchronic cross-section with previous or subsequent structures, one could determine how the literary change in structure (*literarischer Strukturwandel*) is articulated at any time.

Jauss relies on two conceptual aids to develop these points. The first is Siegfried Kracauer's notion of the mixture or coexistence of contemporaneous (*gleichzeitig*) and non-contemporaneous (*ungleichzeitig*) features in any historical mo-ment. This thesis is fruitful for Jauss because it can be used to reinforce the Formalist evolutionary scheme. In any period, the avant-garde constitutes just one movement on the literary scene. A work of "kitsch" or of "normal" literature in that era can be classified then according to the degree of non-contemporaneousness, while those works that are contempor-aneous are presumably associated with the horizon of expecta-tions. Works that properly "belong" to the past are always mixed with those that are genuinely timely in every historical cross-section. The adoption of Kracauer's thesis thus allows

Jauss to explore the historicity of works as a function of the intersection of the diachronic and synchronic planes: "The historicity of literature comes to light exactly at the intersections of diachrony and synchrony" (p. 37).

The other theory Jauss appropriates in part derives from structural linguistics, especially as this was applied to literature by Roman Jakobson and Jurii Tynianov. Literature is viewed by them as a system analogous to a language. Although the researcher uses synchronic methods for heuristic purposes, a pure synchronic description is impossible, since any depiction of a system implies a before and an after. A synchronic method is thus useful only in so far as it assists in locating constant and variable formations within a system. As Jauss observes:

> Literature as well is a kind of grammar or syntax, with relatively fixed relations of its own: the arrangement of the traditional and uncanonized genres; modes of expression, kinds of style, and rhetorical figures; contrasted with this arrangement is the much more variable realm of a semantics: the literary subjects, archetypes, symbols, and metaphors.   (p. 38)

Selecting cross-sections for examination thus provides a means of reading literary history that goes beyond statistical correlations and avoids subjective whim. Instead, the effective-history (*Wirkungsgeschichte*) is the decisive guide for the literary historian, that is, "what results from the event" (*Ereignis*) and what "from the present perspective constitutes the coherence of literature as the prehistory of its present manifestation" (p. 39).

A literary history based on the diachronic and synchronic moments just outlined would still be deficient because it would remain within a literary realm. It could, moreover, foster the notion that literary history can be understood and written independently of social developments. Jauss's final suggestion in his sketch of a reception-oriented history thus endeavors to establish connections between literary production and general history. This problem is actually another version of the central issue in the "Provocation" essay, namely the relationship between aesthetics and history, since for Jauss even the evolutionary series remains essentially an aesthetic construct. The central question of the piece is formulated by Jauss as follows:

If on the one hand literary evolution can be comprehended within the historical change of systems, and on the other hand pragmatic history can be comprehended within the process-like linkage of social conditions, must it not then also be possible to place the "literary series" and the "non-literary series" in a relation that encompasses the relationship between literature and history without forcing literature, at the expense of its character as art, into a function of mere copying or commentary? (p. 18)

Two observations play a role in answering this question. The first concerns the difference between a literary event and a historical occurrence. Comparing Chrétien's *Perceval* with the third crusade – two roughly contemporaneous events – Jauss claims that a literary event does not have the "lasting, unavoidable consequences" associated with political events. It "can continue to have an effect only if those who come after it still or once again respond to it – if there are readers who again appropriate the past work or authors who want to imitate, outdo, or refute it" (p. 22). To use this criterion for distinguishing literature and history, however, is too simple; the consequences of a historical event, indeed, the recognition of any occurrence as an "event," is also dependent on the judgment of "readers" or observers. From the point of view of reception, it appears that this is not a distinction between literary and historical events.

Jauss seems to recognize his error in an article entitled "History of art and pragmatic history" (*Toward an Aesthetic of Reception*, pp. 46–75). In this piece he tries a slightly different strategy to draw the same distinction. He contends:

Literary works differ from purely historical documents precisely because they do more than simply document a particular time, and remain "speaking" to the extent that they attempt to solve problems of form or content, and so extend far beyond the silent relics of the past. (p. 69)

Here Jauss may draw his lines too exclusively. That literature still "speaks" to us does not exclude its documentary character. In fact, it may be its documentary character that allows it to "speak" at all. In drawing this distinction, Jauss tends to situate literature once again in that hermetic realm where timeless values speak to an eternally human condition. Jauss's second manner of dealing with the connection between literary and general history, however, marks one of the most important contributions of his theoretical work. He claims that the previous aesthetics of production and description sought to establish this connection by subordinating literature to history. The former became either a passive reflection of the latter or an example of more general tendencies. Jauss, by contrast, emphasizes the "socially *formative* function of literature" (p. 40). In this context the horizon of expectations assumes a new significance. As a social construct it contains not only literary norms and values, but also desires, demands, and aspirations. The literary work, then, is received and evaluated "against the background of other art forms as well as against the background of the everyday experience of life" (p. 41). In this capacity a work has the possibility of playing an active role in its reception, of calling into question and altering social conventions through both content and form. As an illustration, Jauss cites the famous example of the trial surrounding *Madame Bovary*, where Flaubert was accused of propagating immorality – at least in part due to a misunderstanding of his innovative use of *style indirect libre*. The significance of the artistic device in this case is that it enabled and even demanded a questioning of social mores:

> Since the new artistic device broke through an old novelistic convention – the moral judgment of the represented characters that is always unequivocal and confirmed in the description – the novel was able to radicalize or to raise new questions of lived praxis, which during the proceedings caused the original occasion for the accusation – alleged lasciviousness – to recede wholly into the background.
>
> (p. 43)

With this illustration Jauss wants to call attention to an essential aspect of literature that has been unfortunately neglected by most scholars: literature's effect on society, a matter that, by contrast, has been of utmost concern for writers. Indeed, investigation in this area would accomplish more than just filling in a gap in scholarship. In exploring this aspect of the literary process, researchers would be able to elucidate the emancipatory function of literature while linking the antagonistic terms Jauss has been at pains to reconcile:

> The gap between literature and history, between aesthetic and historical knowledge, can be bridged if literary history does not simply describe the process of general history in the reflection of its works one more time, but rather when it discovers in the course of "literary evolution" that properly *socially formative* function that belongs to literature as it competes with other arts and social forces in the emancipation of mankind from its natural, religious, and social bonds.
>
> (p. 45)

Thus Jauss's provocation, once again emulating his Schillerian model, closes with a plea for emancipation.

Beyond provocation

That Jauss's "Provocation" essay has thus far occupied such a large portion of this section is due in no small part to the chief lessons of reception theory itself. For in West Germany no other essay in literary theory during the past twenty years has received as much attention as this one. It has been the occasion for numerous rebuttals, critiques, and continuations; it has spawned scholarly studies as well as journalistic replies. Indeed, the terminology has even been adopted by non-specialists. As Jauss notes in an essay of the mid-1970s, a newspaper report on soccer contained the following observation: "The interest of the fans is based on a high horizon of expectations."[7] Using the criterion of its own reception as a chief indicator of significance, then, one would have to consider the "Provocation" essay the most significant document of German literary theory in the last few decades.

The far-reaching effects of this piece, however, have possibly had greater consequences for other scholars than for Jauss himself; for the appearance of *Literary History as Provocation* in 1970 marks a pivotal point in his theoretical work. Thereafter his interests have turned away from those which inspired his provocative manifesto. He retains the concern for history in his subsequent work as well as the emphasis on investigating the interaction between audience and texts. But in the 1970s there is a diminished role allotted to the Russian Formalists. Their views on perception and defamiliarization as well as the evolutionary model of literary history recede into the background and are mentioned only infrequently. Gone too, for the most part, is the seminal concept of the horizon of expectations. Although Jauss continues to apply this category in some of the individual analyses of works and their reception, it is noteworthy that the term crops up rarely in the central theoretical essays in his major book of this period: *Aesthetic Experience and Literary Hermeneutics*.[8] Indeed, if there is a major shift in Jauss's overall position, it can be seen as early as 1972 in the pamphlet *Kleine Apologie der ästhetischen Erfahrung* (Small Apology for Aesthetic Experience).[9] For already in this work the horizon of expectations and the Russian Formalist influence are noticeably reduced.

The "aesthetics of negativity"

The reason for this implicit repudiation of his earlier theoretical work seems to be connected with a more general devaluation of what Jauss refers to as the "aesthetics of negativity." Reacting to the posthumous publication of Theodor Adorno's *Aesthetic Theory* in 1970[10] – for Jauss the paradigm of a negative theory of art – he reconsiders the implications of his own "negativity" as well.

What bothers Jauss about Adorno's theory is that it allows a positive social function for art only when the artwork negates the specific society in which it is produced. It thereby leaves no room for an affirmative *and* progressive literature, since literature in general is defined by its opposition to social practices, by its "ascetic" character. Moreover, such a theory tends to promote an élitist, avant-garde concept of art through its valorization of the non-communicative function of genuine culture. Only art that stubbornly affirms its autonomy in the face of a reified culture, that becomes a "scheme of social praxis" by removing itself from praxis (p. 349), and that severs its ties with "normal" language and images, can be, according to Adorno, authentic art. Even those artists who seem to fall outside of this paradigm are forced to fit a pattern of social estrangement: "In artists of the highest order, like Beethoven or Rembrandt, the most acute consciousness of reality is combined with alienation from reality" (p. 21).

Perhaps even more objectionable for Jauss, though, is the radical separation Adorno postulates between art and pleasure (*Genuss*) or happiness:

> Taking subjective pleasure [*Lust*] in a work of art would approach the state of that which is released from empirical experience as the totality of the being-for-another, not empirical experience itself. Schopenhauer was probably the first to have realized this. Happiness in encountering a work of art is the condition of having suddenly escaped, not a morsel of that from which art emanated; it is always only accidental, less essential for art than happiness of its cognition; the concept of artistic pleasure [*Kunstgenuss*] as constitutive should be abolished. (p. 30)

Adorno's notion of art, Jauss claims, avoids a confrontation with the primary function of art throughout the ages. It is unable to appreciate the artistic value of a wide range of literary works, from medieval heroic epics to the classics of "affirmative" literature. Caught in a machine of perpetual negativity, Adorno's aesthetics winds up preaching an élitist puritanism that effectively severs art from any but the most indirect formative role.

Adorno shares this negativity with many other theories of art and literature in the twentieth century. The aesthetics Jauss identifies with the *Tel Quel* group, for example, is subjected to a similar, though less extensive critique. The one-sided heritage of the nineteenth century, summarized in the formula *l'art pour l'art*, survives in the "materialist" aesthetics of this group in the valorization of works that stand in irreconcilable contradiction to social hegemony. But the uncompromising posture of this theory is purchased only at the price of a total absence of efficacy.

> One cannot see how, with recipes of pure negativity, that is, recipes that deny identification with the social condition – which is also the greatest wisdom for a negative aesthetics like that of the *Tel Quel* group – a new scheme of social praxis could be grounded. (*Apologie*, p. 47)

This one-sidedness is also associated now with the theories of the Russian Formalists. The exclusive attention to innovative accomplishments, to defamiliarizing perception, although it does not necessarily sever the connection between literature and social effect, assumes that literature is perceived and valued only against a normal or automatized societal and/or literary background. Russian Formalism, then, perpetuates a variety of the same negativity found in Adorno or the *Tel Quel* group.

But so does a reception theory based on the breaking of horizons of expectations. Jauss recognizes this weakness in his earlier work when he admits the partial nature of his former depiction of aesthetic experience. In the first place, by excluding primary aesthetic experience, the aesthetics of reception shared an artistic asceticism with other contemplative and self-reflexive modes of speculation (p. 55).[11] And secondly, through the orientation on autonomous art (for Jauss, roughly art in the post-Romantic era), it ignored not only the important role of pre-autonomous art, but also the variety of functions that art has had and potentially has:

> According to this theory [the aesthetics of reception] the essence of the artwork is based on its historicity, that is, on the effect resulting from its continuous dialogue with the public; the relationship between art and society had to be grasped in the dialectic of question and answer; and the history of art acquires its uniqueness in the change in horizon between natural tradition and comprehending reception, delayed classicism and the continuous formation of the canon. It shares with the evolution theory of the Formalists as well as with the aesthetics of negativity and all theories directed towards emancipation (the Marxists included) the conviction of the primacy of the eventfully new [*des ereignishaften Neuen*] against that which has resulted from the process [*das prozesshafte Gewordensein*], the negativity or difference against affirmative or institutionalized meaning. These premises are adequate for the history and social role of art after it has reached autonomy; but they cannot . . . do justice to its practical, communicative, and norm-constituting function in the area of pre-autonomous art. (*Apologie*, pp. 50–1)

The central theses in the "Provocation" essay thus retain only a limited validity as early as 1972. In effect Jauss here removes the horizon of expectations from the center of his aesthetics. For if only autonomous art can be adequately comprehended through negativity, then the breaking of expectations does not represent an aesthetic norm, but only one special case in a longer and more complex history of aesthetic experiencing.

Reintroducing pleasure

What Jauss opposes to this aesthetics of negativity is primary aesthetic experience. He reminds us of the simple fact that most contact with art has been occasioned by *Genuss*. This word has two meanings in German, and Jauss wants to include both in his concept. In the most common usage today *Genuss* can be translated by pleasure or enjoyment; an older sense of the word, however, would bring it into the word field of use or utility. The verb form for the word, *geniessen*, as Jauss points out, was used commonly in the eighteenth century to designate "to make use of something."

In both of these senses, *Genuss* has been the seminal inspiration for interest in art, even if it has been virtually ignored by the aesthetic tradition. Perhaps most important for us is its decline in importance during the past two centuries. While aesthetic experience was once considered to possess a legitimate cognitive and communicative function, more recent art and theory have stripped it of these roles and consigned pleasure to cultural attitudes associated with the narrow-minded, pretentious middle classes.

> Now shorn of its cognitive and communicative efficacy, aesthetic pleasure appears either as the sentimental or utopian opposite of alienation in the three-phase models of the philosophy of history or, in contemporary aesthetic theory, as the essence of an attitude that is considered philistine when adopted toward classical art and simply excluded vis-à-vis modern art.   (p. 26)

Jauss's ambition is to challenge this tradition by restoring primary aesthetic experience to its rightful place at the center of literary theory.

Twentieth-century theory, or course, has not completely

ignored the problem of pleasure and art. Perhaps the most celebrated recent writer to treat this problem in a positive light was Roland Barthes in *The Pleasure of the Text* (1973).[12] But Jauss takes issue with Barthes because of his alleged adherence to an aesthetics of negativity. Although Barthes is credited with refuting the simplistic notion that all aesthetic pleasure is an instrument of the ruling class and thus condemnable, his separation of aesthetic experience into *plaisir* and *jouissance* – for affirmative and negative aesthetic pleasure respectively – reintroduces the ambivalence towards art that has informed criticism since Plato. Ultimately, Jauss contends, Barthes's book supports only the pleasure of the scholar:

> It is no accident that Barthes's apology reduces aesthetic pleasure [*Lust*] to the pleasure [*Vergnügen*] that lies in the commerce with language. Since he fails to open the self-sufficient linguistic universe with enough decisiveness toward the world of aesthetic practice, his highest happiness ultimately remains the rediscovered eros of the contemplative philologist and his undisturbed preserve: "the paradise of words." (p. 30)

To avoid the deleterious consequence of negative aesthetics Jauss takes a somewhat different approach. Pleasure, understood as the opposite of work, but not necessarily in contradiction to action or cognition, must be separated from aesthetic pleasure phenomenologically. Drawing on Ludwig Giesz's appropriation of Moritz Geiger's work on aesthetic pleasure, but also on Sartre's discussion of the imaginary, Jauss determines that aesthetic pleasure consists of two moments. In the first, which is also applicable to all pleasure, there occurs an unmediated surrender (*Hingabe*) of the ego to the object. The second moment, which is peculiar to aesthetic pleasure, consists of "the taking up of a position that brackets the existence of the object and thereby makes it an aesthetic one" (pp. 30–1). An aesthetic attitude thus includes a distancing of the observer from the object, and this aesthetic distancing is for Jauss simultaneously a creative act of consciousness: in aesthetic contemplation the observer produces an imaginary object. Giesz describes this experiencing of the aesthetic as a hovering between primary pleasure and its object. In Kantian terms one might think of a movement between subject and object in which we acquire an "interest in our disinterestedness" (p. 32). Jauss endeavors to capture aesthetic enjoyment, however, in the formula "self-enjoyment in the enjoyment of something other" (*Selbstgenuss im Fremdgenuss*).

Productive aesthetic experience: "poiesis"

With this expression Jauss wants to emphasize not only the back-and-forth movement between subject and object, but also the "primary unity of understanding enjoyment and enjoying understanding" (p. 32). Pleasure, in other words, should not be separated from its cognitive and praxis-oriented functions, and it is with this concept of aesthetic experience in mind that Jauss proceeds to analyze historically the three "fundamental categories" of aesthetic pleasure: *poiesis*, *aisthesis*, and *catharsis*.

The first of these categories refers to the productive side of aesthetic experience, the pleasure that stems from the application of one's own creative abilities. What interests Jauss most in his discussion of this concept is the evolution it has undergone from ancient to modern times. According to the Aristotelian hierarchy of knowledge, *poiesis* as productive action remained subordinated to practical activity or *praxis* in the ancient and the medieval world. Nevertheless, it was an ability that was capable of being perfected (pp. 46–7). The change in world views in the modern era contributed to a concomitant alteration in the notion of *poiesis*. Instead of referring to the ability to imitate a pre-existing perfection, it gradually became identified with creating a work that itself would bring forth perfection, or at least the beautiful appearance (*schöner Schein*) of completion (p. 49). Using Leonardo da Vinci as presented by Paul Valéry as a prototype for this conception of *poiesis*, Jauss points to its constructive aspect, which is more than the mere imitation of the truth; *poiesis* here is a "cognition dependent on what one can do, on a form of action that tries and tests so that understanding and producing can become one" (p. 51).

The last step towards autonomy implied in this Renaissance rendition of *poiesis* – creation of perfection rather than reproduction – was taken by the "literary revolution in the eighteenth century" (p. 52). By the nineteenth century, the work of art becomes the paradigm for a non-alienated activity, especially in

Marx's early writings. The change that Jauss notes in the twentieth century involves *poiesis* becoming a function of the audience as much as the artist. With the demise of the metaphysics of eternal beauty, art has become defined by ambiguity and indeterminacy. The artwork becomes an *objet ambigu*, to use Paul Valéry's term, whose construction and cognition depend on the receiver or observer as well as the producer. In this way Jauss again historicizes his own earlier aesthetics of reception, which is now depicted as a theory adequate to and necessary for dealing with only this altered notion of *poiesis*.

Receptive aesthetic experience: aisthesis

The dependence of *poiesis* on reception in modern art means that it converges in recent times with the second category of Jauss's aesthetic trinity, *aisthesis*. Defined as aesthetic perception, it refers to the receptive side of aesthetic experience. To outline its history, Jauss proceeds to examine a number of exemplary texts in which observation and perception, especially the contemplation of nature, play an important role. In this manner he hopes to circumvent or at least to minimize the hermeneutical problem of trying to perceive what the history of perception has been.

In the ancient world, where aesthetic and theoretical curiosity were not yet separated, *aisthesis* entailed a presentation of events in the double sense of portraying and making present. Since the ancients did not draw an ontological distinction between an earlier and a later occurrence, there was no ranking or hierarchy of moments in this presentation. In the scenes described on Achilles's shield, which Jauss takes as his illustrative case, each picture contains its own beauty. "As the pleasurable lingering in the presence of a perfect manifestation, *aisthesis* here expresses its highest concept" (p. 67). In contrast, the *aisthesis* of the Christian Middle Ages is subsumed under the formula of the "poetry of the invisible," since here the difference between figure and significance constitutes the primary receptive experience.

With Petrarch, according to Jauss, we can already detect the beginnings of a new form of *aisthesis*: on the one hand, the internal workings of the soul and, on the other hand, the beauty of the natural world become increasingly important for the receptive side of aesthetic experience. The most significant impetus to this process of changing *aisthesis* comes with the separation of science and aesthetics: the former, in its modern role of categorizer of natural phenomena, no longer deals with the experience of the totality of nature, and this function is ceded to aesthetics.

The culmination of this development, however, occurs during the Romantic movement. With the inversion of the Augustinian scheme of this-worldly renunciation, landscape and autobiography become the two poles that perhaps best capture the span of the new *aisthesis*. But the increased importance of contemplating external nature should not be understood as an "unmediated enjoyment of what is at hand" (p. 81), as it had been in the ancient world. Rather, as Schiller indicates with his concept of the sentimental, it is now a nostalgic sentiment for a lost naïveté. Romantic *aisthesis* thus gives rise to a new type of experience in the form of remembrance, and this incipient discovery of the *aisthetic* faculty of memory then serves as a bridge to the most recent alterations in receptive experience.

These modern forms of *aisthesis* are presented by Jauss as two competing variants. One has a critical linguistic function and is associated with Flaubert, Valéry, Beckett, and Robbe-Grillet, while the other possesses a "cosmological" function (one might also say "communal" or "species") and is identified with Baudelaire and Proust. The former variant, according to Jauss, has the tendency to destroy or to call into question all *aisthesis* as well as communication in general; thus it potentially annihilates all possibility of aesthetic experience. In keeping with his general dissatisfaction with an aesthetics of negativity, to which this tendency is related, he therefore attempts to discredit this branch of the modern tradition while simultaneously holding up Proust's theory as exemplary and preferable. What he finds so attractive in Proust is the reintroduction of the epistemological function of *aisthesis* through the romantically mediated category of memory. Indeed, Jauss sees a basic trend since the middle of the nineteenth century concerned with a reacquisition of the cognitive role of art. In contrast to the popular notion that art has diminished in importance, he postulates that the tasks assigned to aesthetic experience have never been greater:

In this process aesthetic experience at the level of *aisthesis* took on a task vis-à-vis the growing alienation of social existence which had never previously been set for it in the history of the arts: to counter the shrunken experience and subservient language of the "cultural industry" by the linguistically critical and creative function of aesthetic perception. In view of the pluralism of social roles and scientific perspectives, such perception was also to preserve the experience of the world others have and thus to safeguard a common horizon which, the cosmological whole being gone, art can most readily sustain.   (p. 92)

In Jauss's scheme, art and the aesthetic experience which it allows contain not only an immanent socially critical moment, but also a solidifying aspect for a society that has lost touch with its own experiences. By providing for common perceptions, *aisthesis* becomes the glue that holds together the most diverse and alienated elements in a modern technological world.

Communicative aesthetic experience: catharsis

The third and final category that is constitutive of the history of aesthetic experiences is *catharsis*, which is understood as the communicative component between art and recipient. Although Jauss explicates this category in his central theoretical piece by tracing the fate of Aristotle's controversial term from the ancients to Brecht, perhaps a more enlightening discussion of the communicative side of art is found in his essay on "Interactive patterns of identification with the hero." In Jauss's view, an important aspect of communication takes place in transmitting role models for behavior, and *catharsis* can therefore be examined in part through an analysis of aesthetic identification.

It would be false, of course, to consider aesthetic identification as a passive receiving on the part of the audience. Rather, like all communicative processes, it entails a "back-and-forth movement between the aesthetically freed observer and his irreal object in which the subject in its aesthetic enjoyment can run through an entire scale of attitudes" (p. 94). The heuristic model of heroic types that Jauss constructs should thus serve as part of a larger project involving aesthetically mediated patterns of identification. But perhaps just as important, basing this model on the variety of interactive patterns between art and audience again points to one of the chief deficiencies of the aesthetics of negativity. By excluding identification as a primary aesthetic experience and allowing for only the ironic breaking of norms or the banal, mass-cultural affirmation of expectations, theoreticians of negativity neglect an entire realm of aesthetic phenomena. Jauss, in contrast, is concerned with the gamut of identification patterns, and one might therefore understand his project here as an attempt to fill in the vast space between the two extremes validated by the aesthetics of negativity.

Jauss identifies five patterns of interaction, which appear in summary form in the table on p. 80. In contrast to Northrop Frye's typology of heroes in *Anatomy of Criticism* (1957),[13] these categories are based on modalities of reception, not on the actions or utterances of the figures.

Although there is a rough chronological sequence to this typology, each pattern can be found in all societies and several may occur in a single work. Associative identification, for example, while generally encountered in less developed social organizations, can be seen as well in forms of medieval courtly etiquette or, in more recent times, in the living-theater or happenings. What is decisive for this modality is an active participation by the spectator, the breaking down of the barrier between actors and audience. Associative identification entails "assuming a role in the closed, imaginary world of a play action" (p. 164). Admiring identification, on the other hand, involves a perfect hero whose actions are exemplary for a community or a segment of the community. Although the most obvious illustrations of this type of interaction are contained in medieval epics, both heroic and courtly, numerous examples come to mind from other eras as well (Jauss mentions *La Nouvelle Héloïse* and *Werther*).

The third modality, sympathetic identification, can often be the result of initial admiration. In this type of interaction the audience places itself in the position of the hero and thus expresses a kind of solidarity with a usually suffering figure. The cathartic identification, by contrast, is characterized by its

Modality of identification	Reference	Receptive disposition	Norms of behavior or attitude (+ = positive, − = negative)
I. Associative	Game/competition (ceremony)	Placing oneself in the roles of all other participants	+ Enjoyment of free existence (pure sociability) − Collective fascination (regression into archaic rituals)
II. Admiring	The perfect hero (saint, sage)	Admiration	+ Aemulatio (emulation) − Imitatio (imitation) + Exemplariness − Edification or entertainment by way of the extraordinary (need for escape)
III. Sympathetic	The imperfect (everyday) hero	Pity	+ Moral interest (readiness to act) − Sentimentality (enjoyment of pain) + Solidarity for the sake of definite action − Self-confirmation (soothing)
IV. Cathartic	(a) The suffering hero	Tragic emotional up-heaval/inner liberation	+ Disinterested interest, free reflection − Lurid fascination (pleasure in illusion)
	(b) The hard-pressed hero	Sympathetic laughter/comic inner release	+ Free moral judgment − Derision (laugh-ritual)
V. Ironic	The missing hero or anti-hero	Alienation (provoca-tion)	+ Reciprocal creativity − Solipsism + Refinement of perception − Cultivated boredom + Critical reflection − Indifference

Table 1: Interactional patterns of aesthetic identification with the hero

Source: Hans Robert, *Aesthetic Experience* (1982: p. 152)

emancipatory function for the spectator. Occurring in both tragic and comic situations, this modality involves aesthetic distance: "The spectator is allowed the tragic emotion or sympathetic laughter only to the extent that he is capable of detaching himself from the immediacy of his identification and rises to judgment and reflection about what is represented" (p. 178). Finally, the ironic modality entails disappointing, breaking, or denying an expected identification. This familiar and, in recent times, privileged interactive model is most often encountered in parody and modernist literature. It is exemplary not only for an aesthetics of negativity, but also for Jauss's own earlier aesthetics of reception; that it here occupies only a fraction of his "heuristic model" should again serve as an indication of the distance between Jauss's initial "provocation" and his later work.

The provocation of literary theory

Indeed, one might read Jauss's occupation with aesthetic experience in general as a revision of his initial hypotheses about reception. While quite a few of the more questionable statements were eliminated or altered, his latest theoretical framework incorporates in a partial fashion several aspects of the horizon of expectations. This self-critical attitude on Jauss's part is not only admirable, but has served to strengthen his theoretical positions.

Yet compared to his aesthetics of reception, this more recent work has failed to provoke anything near the same degree and intensity of response. And this relative absence of response cannot be attributed totally to a less provocative hypothesis. After all, the main contention in turning to investigations of aesthetic experience is that a good deal of the history of speculation on art has been far removed from the fundamental manner in which art functions and is enjoyed in real life. The sharp criticisms of the aesthetics of negativity associated with Adorno and French theory also seem designed to provoke reaction from partisan corners. Perhaps part of the lack of response can be attributed to more formal features in Jauss's recent work. In *Aesthetic Experience and Literary Hermeneutics* the style has become drier, more academic. Although he displays a tremendous range in both his literary allusions and theoretical sources, this erudition can be a barrier rather than an aid to reception.

But probably the chief reason for the failure of Jauss's work to ignite the German critical community as it once did is that the constituency and mood of that community have altered dramatically. No longer are students concerned with participating in a theoretical revolution. No longer are literary scholars eager to make the study of literature relevant again. And no longer are the universities as a system involved with innovation and upheaval. In this climate a theory of aesthetic experience, however novel and necessary, is just another academic enterprise. Its reception, no matter how provocatively postured, is restricted, as Jauss himself had demonstrated earlier, by factors beyond its control.[14]

Textuality and the reader's response: Wolfgang Iser

The reception of Wolfgang Iser's work was also determined largely by general cultural factors, and to an extent it parallels the response to Jauss's writings. His most successful early piece, "Die Appellstruktur der Texte" (1970), which appeared in English as "Indeterminacy and the Reader's Response in Prose Fiction," was originally a lecture delivered at the University of Constance, where Iser also teaches.[1] The impact of this talk and its printed version, although perhaps not as intense or protracted as the reaction to Jauss's "Provocation," established Iser as one of the foremost theorists of the "Constance School." His major theoretical volume, however, did not appear until the mid-1970s, and, like Jauss's *Aesthetic Experience, The Act of Reading* (1976)[2] did not arouse quite as much controversy as the less finished, but more explosive lecture.

But these similarities in the German reception of the "dioscuri" of reception theory should not obscure their fundamental differences. Although both have been concerned with a reconstitution of literary theory by drawing attention away from the author and the text and refocusing it on the text–reader relationship, their respective methods of approaching this shift have diverged sharply. While the Romance-scholar Jauss was initially moved towards reception theory through his concern for literary history, Iser, a scholar of English literature, comes from the interpretative orientations of New Criticism and narrative theory. Whereas Jauss depended at first on hermeneutics and was particularly influenced by Hans-Georg Gadamer, the major impact on Iser has been phenomenology. Particularly important in this regard has been the work of Roman Ingarden, from whom Iser adopts his basic model as well as a number of key concepts. Finally, even in his later work Jauss is most often interested in issues of a broad social and historical nature. His examination of the history of aesthetic experience, for example, is developed in a grand historical sweep in which individual works have chiefly an illustrative function. Iser, by contrast, is concerned primarily with the individual text and how readers relate to it. Although he does not exclude social and historical factors, they are clearly subordinated to or incorporated in more detailed textual considerations. If one thinks of Jauss as dealing with the macrocosm of reception, then Iser occupies himself with the microcosm of response (*Wirkung*).

The production of meaning

One additional difference is perhaps relevant for the presentation of Iser's views. While Jauss appears to have renounced or at least to have pushed aside large portions of his earlier thought, Iser's theory can be more profitably understood as an expansion of his initial premises. Indeed, most of the central notions and examples in the "Appellstruktur" essay are incorporated into *The Act of Reading*. Iser's contribution to literary theory can therefore be more easily discussed as a coherent and continuous development, an elaboration rather than a correction of his early work, and for this reason a consideration of his major theoretical volume provides the best method for exploring his contribution to reception theory over the past decade and a half.

What has interested Iser from the outset is the question of how and under what conditions a text has meaning for a reader. In contrast to traditional interpretation, which has sought to elucidate a hidden meaning in the text, he wants to see meaning as the result of an interaction between text and reader, as "an effect to be experienced," not an "object to be defined" (p. 10). Ingarden's conception of the literary work of art thus provides a useful framework for his investigations. For if the aesthetic object is constituted only through an act of cognition on the part of the reader, then the focus is switched from the text as object to the act of reading as process.

The literary work is neither completely text nor completely the subjectivity of the reader, but a combination or merger of the two. Accordingly Iser maps out three domains for exploration. The first involves the text in its potential to allow and manipulate the production of meaning. Like Ingarden, Iser regards the text as a skeleton of "schematized aspects" that must be actualized or concretized by the reader. Second, he investigates the processing of the text in reading. Of central importance here are the mental images formed when attempting to construct a consistent and cohesive aesthetic object. Finally, he turns to the communicatory structure of literature to examine the conditions that give rise to and govern the text–reader interaction. In considering these three areas Iser hopes to clarify not only how meaning is produced, but also what effects literature has on its reader.

The implied reader

To describe the interaction between text and reader Iser introduces a number of concepts borrowed or adapted from other theorists. Perhaps the most controversial of these has been the "implied reader." This term, which comprises the title of a volume of Iser's essays on prose fiction,[3] is evidently a counterpart to Wayne Booth's concept of the implied author as elaborated in *The Rhetoric of Fiction* (1961).[4] In the book that bears its name, the implied reader is defined as both a textual condition and a process of meaning production: "The term incorporates both the prestructuring of the potential meaning by the text, and the reader's actualization of this potential through the reading process" (*The Implied Reader*, p. xii). Iser thereby endeavors to distinguish it from the various categories and typologies of readers that have arisen in recent years. In *The Act of Reading* the rationale for defining the term in such an odd fashion is more easily discernible. What Iser wants is a way to account for the reader's presence without having to deal with real or empirical readers, as well as the various abstract readers, whose characters have been predetermined – Riffaterre's "superreader" or Fish's "informal reader," for example. In other words, he seeks a "transcendental model" (p. 38), what might also be called a "phenomenological reader," one that "embodies all those predispositions necessary for a literary work to exercise its effect" (p. 34), while precluding empirical interference.

In bracketing the real reader and any predispositions, however, Iser often comes dangerously close to defining his "construct" in purely literary terms. The roots of the implied reader, we are told, are "firmly planted in the structure of the text." And at one point Iser even writes that his concept is "a textual structure anticipating the presence of a recipient without necessarily defining him" (p. 34). But if the implied reader were purely textual, it would be synonymous with the structure of appeal (*Appellstruktur*) of a literary work, and to call it a "reader" at all would be senseless, if not downright misleading. The bifunctionality of this concept, as both "textual structure" and "structured act," is thus essential if the term is to escape a purely immanent meaning. Yet by introducing this dual definition Iser may not accomplish his intentions either. Although his supporters can very well account for this sort of doubling as the unavoidable result of a sophisticated endeavor to grasp process, his detractors can just as easily point to the consequences of the haziness of this designation. For defining the term in this fashion allows him to move to and fro from text to reader without ever clarifying the composition and contribution of either half of this partnership. The implied reader may evidence a deficiency in rigor rather than an abundance of sophistication.

Fiction and reality: the structure of the text

Iser may have been sensitive to the problems with the implied reader in *The Act of Reading*. While in the second chapter the term is offered as an alternative to competing constructs in other reader-oriented theories, it is rarely mentioned during the rest of the volume. Instead Iser turns to an investigation of precisely the two poles that the implied reader was supposed to span: the text and the reading process. Literature, which Iser identifies with fiction, is not to be seen as an opposition to reality; rather, it is "a means of telling us something about reality" (p. 53). It does this by placing the reader in a communicative situation that is likened to the illocutionary act described in speech-act theory by J. L. Austin and John Searle. This division of linguistic utterance is defined in terms of performance rather than meaning. In Austin's theory the illocutionary act may involve any one of a number of common activities: promising, informing, ordering, threatening, warning, etc. What is essential, though, is that it has a potential effect or an "illocutionary force" and invites an appropriate response on the part of the recipient. Assuming sincerity on the part of the speaker and provided that the speaker and the recipient share the same conventions and procedures, the latter comprehends the force of the speech act, and hence its "meaning," from the situational context. For Iser there are obvious parallels with literary language:

> The language of literature resembles the mode of the illocutionary act, but has a different function. As we have seen, the success of a linguistic action depends on the resolution of indeterminacies by means of conventions, procedures, and guarantees of sincerity. These form the frame of reference within which the speech act can be resolved into a context of action. Literary texts also require a resolution of indeterminacies but, by definition, for fiction there can be no such given frames of reference. On the contrary, the reader must first discover for himself the code underlying the text, and this is tantamount to bringing out the meaning.   (p. 60)

The distinguishing feature of literature is thus that it deals with conventions in a different manner. While "normal" speech acts validate conventions in utilizing past communicative practices for comprehension, fiction calls conventions into question. Speech acts organize conventions "vertically" from past to present; literary speech acts combine conventions "horizontally." "As a result these conventions are taken out of their social contexts, deprived of their regulating function, and so become subjects of scrutiny in themselves" (p. 61). Literature "tells us something about reality" by ordering its conventions so that they become objects of our reflection.

Iser refers to these conventions as the repertoire of the text. It is the "familiar territory" on which text and reader meet to initiate communication. But if the repertoire were totally familiar, the text would not fulfill its imputed function of communicating something new to the reader. Through the repertoire, therefore, the literary text reorganizes social and cultural norms as well as literary traditions so that the reader may reassess their function in real life. A text should be understood as "a reaction to the thought systems which it has chosen and incorporated in its own repertoire" (p. 72). For literature provides possibilities that have been "excluded by the prevalent system" (p. 73), enabling readers "to see what they cannot normally see in the ordinary process of day-to-day living" (p. 74). The repertoire thus assumes a dual function in Iser's model: "it reshapes familiar schemata to form a background for the process of communication, and it provides a general framework within which the message or meaning of the text can be organized" (p. 81).

With the notion of the repertoire Iser comes closest to Jauss's earlier aesthetics of reception. In defining a "prevailing system" – whether social or literary – against which the reorganized repertoire is perceived and has an effect, he recalls his colleague's hypothesis of a horizon of expectations that is broken or disappointed by literary works. But if Iser indeed insists that literature "takes its selected objects out of their pragmatic contexts and so shatters their original frame of reference" (p. 109), he too falls victim to what Jauss has labeled the aesthetics of negativity – despite his own criticism of the "deviationist model" (pp. 87–92). Although he may wish to conceive of the text as allowing "an extension or broadening" of the reader's reality (p. 79), it does so only because it is viewed *against* that reality, as deviation, innovation, or negation. For this reason his theory displays the characteristic difficulty of accounting for the "affirmative" literature of the Middle Ages, and he is ultimately compelled to regard the greater part of this tradition as "trivial" (pp. 77–8).

He also has a problem in determining why modern readers are interested in older works and what they derive from them. By constructing his system around readers contemporary with a given text and its repertoire, he excludes all but intellectual curiosity as motivation: while the reader contemporary with the work gains insights into the organization of his/her own world, the current "observer" will simply "grasp something which has hitherto never been real for him" (p. 79). That according to this criterion a pot-boiler from the past would perform exactly the same function as a "masterpiece" indicates the unresolved nature of this issue in Iser's speculations.

The repertoire includes mostly elements that have been traditionally considered "content." As such, it needs a form or structure to organize its presentation, and Iser adopts the term "strategies" to designate this function. Because he is concerned with the interaction of text and reader, however, Iser does not want us to think of the strategies as mere structural features. Rather, they entail both the ordering of materials and the conditions under which those materials are communicated. In Iser's words, they encompass both "the immanent structure of the text and the acts of comprehension thereby triggered off in the reader" (p. 86).

Now these strategies should not be understood as a total organization; for in this case the reader would not have any organizational role to play. Nor should they be viewed as traditional narrative techniques or rhetorical devices; for these, according to Iser, are only surface phenomena of the text. What he means by strategies is, instead, the structures that underlie such superficial techniques and allow them to have an effect.

Keeping in mind that the "ultimate function of the strategies is to *defamiliarize* the familiar" (p. 87), Iser outlines two governing structures: foreground and background, and theme and horizon. The first of these pairs refers to the relationship that permits certain elements to stand out while others recede into a general context. Similar to the figure-and-ground distinction in *Gestalt* psychology, it steers the perceptions of the reader and is responsible for the "meaning" of the literary work.

> The background–foreground relation is a basic structure by means of which the strategies of the text produce a tension that sets off a series of different actions and interactions, and that is ultimately resolved by the emergence of the aesthetic object.   (p. 95)

The terms "theme" and "horizon," which Iser borrows from Alfred Schütz's phenomenological theory, involve the selection from multiple perspectives in a text. In most narratives, Iser

sees four vantage points: "that of the narrator, that of the
characters, that of the plot, and that marked out for the reader"
(p. 96). When the reader is concerned with any one of these
perspectives, his/her attitude will be conditioned by the horizon
established from past reading and the other perspectives. The
tension between theme and horizon thus creates a "mechanism
that regulates perception," although the "ultimate meaning of
the text" necessarily transcends any individual perspective (p.
98). Iser also suggests that a typology of perspectival arrangements can be built on the various constellations of theme and
horizon. In pre-modern literature, for example, he identifies a
"counterbalancing" structure typical of didactic and devotion-
al literature. Here the strategy is to limit alternatives so that the
reader is forced into a simple and obvious choice. Slightly more
sophisticated is the "oppositional" arrangement in which the
switching perspectives compel the reader to question the norms
of each point of view. In general, this strategy appears in liberal
enlightenment novels like *Tom Jones* or *Humphry Clinker*.

During the past century, on the other hand, one more frequently encounters "echelon" and "serial" arrangements. Both
of these strategies preclude a positive orientation by constantly
undercutting any perspective or guidelines. The serial structure, which Iser identifies with Joyce's *Ulysses* and the *nouveau
roman*, accelerates the alteration of theme and horizon to such an
extent that reference itself becomes problematized. These different applications of theme-and-horizon arrangements,
therefore, represent textual strategies that order – even if the
goal is disorientation – the reader's perceptions of elements
in the repertoire, enabling the production of an appropriate
aesthetic object.

Processing the text: a phenomenology of reading

To complement the repertoire and strategies that make up the
functionalist model of a literary text, Iser develops a concomitant phenomenology of reading. Of central importance for this
phenomenology is the concept of the "wandering viewpoint."
Conceived as "a means of describing the way in which the
reader is present in the text" (p. 118), it is meant to overcome
the external reader–text relationship; for the unique quality of

literature, according to Iser, is that the object is grasped from the "inside." The journey of the wandering viewpoint may be best understood by considering what Iser calls the "dialectic of protension and retention" (p. 112).

Adopted from Husserl's discussion of temporality, these terms refer to the "modified expectations" and "transformed memories" that inform the reading process. When we read a text, we are continuously evaluating and perceiving events with regard to our expectations for the future and against the background of the past. An unexpected occurrence will therefore cause us to reformulate our expectations in accordance with this event and to reinterpret the significance we have attributed to what has already occurred. The wandering viewpoint thus "permits the reader to travel through the text . . . unfolding the multiplicity of interconnecting perspectives which are offset whenever there is a switch from one to another" (p. 118).

The assumption behind this description of the reading process is labeled "consistency-building." In confronting the various signs or schemata of a text, readers try to establish connections between them that lend coherence to their activity. Iser assumes that a reader will form *Gestalten* in the process of participating in meaning-production. If something occurs that is at odds with an imagined *Gestalt*, then the reader will endeavor to make things consistent again through a series of revisions. Indeed, the "dialectic between illusion-making and illusion-breaking" as well as the related "oscillation between involvement and observation" are fundamental for the constitution of the aesthetic object and account for the experience of the text as a "living event" (pp. 127–8). Even if the intent of the text is to deny consistency – as one might encounter in a modern novel – the reader involved in the production of this meaning will arrive at this conclusion only by means of the principle of consistency-building.

A second area that Iser explores in connection with the reading process is the image-making activity of the reader. While we read, we are continuously and unconsciously constructing images in a process Iser calls "passive synthesis" (p. 135). These images should be distinguished from perceptions we have when encountering empirical reality; for the image "transcends" the sensory. It is something which accompanies reading, something "not yet fully conceptualized" (p. 136). Here Iser is drawing on the difference between the German words for perception (*Wahrnehmung*) and ideation (*Vorstellung*). The former occurs only when an object is present to be perceived, while the latter presupposes the absence or non-existence of an object. Reading entails ideation because, aside from the marks on the page, the reader must bring forth or ideate the "object," usually thought of in terms of a world suggested by the "schematized aspects" of the text. Ideation, in other words, is an essential part of the creative imagination that ultimately produces an aesthetic object. It does not always accomplish this in a straightforward manner, of course. On the contrary, in most non-trivial works, images are produced and recede again, being modified and reconstituted in a complex temporal process. Meaning, as an end result of this process, thus consists of a synthesis of various phases, and since the images can never be precisely duplicated, it is never exactly the same.

But perhaps Iser's most suggestive comments on reading concern the effect on the subject. In contrast to Poulet's "substantialist concept of consciousness," which relies on a subject–object distinction in identifying each text with a consciousness, Iser posits a bifurcation of the subject in reading. When we appropriate an alien experience foregrounded in the text, we simultaneously background our own previous experiences. In assimilating the other, we alienate part of ourselves. "The division, then, is not between subject and object, but between subject and himself" (p. 155). Since we bring forth this "alien" meaning, however, it should be more accurately viewed as part of our hitherto unrecognized consciousness. Understood in this way, reading really effects a "heightening of self-awareness which develops in the reading process" (p. 157). And it is this therapeutic, almost psychoanalytic consequence of our encounter with texts that Iser deems significant as meaning-production:

> The constitution of meaning not only implies the creation of a totality emerging from interacting textual perspectives . . . but also, through formulating this totality, it enables us to formulate ourselves and thus discover an inner world of which we had hitherto not been conscious. (p. 158)

Reading becomes a medium through which consciousness comes to realize itself.

Literature and communication:
interaction between text and reader

After analyzing the reading process and the text from a phe-nomenological and functional perspective respectively, Iser turns to the communicatory structure of fiction. Starting from the "normal," face-to-face communicatory situation in which two equal partners endeavor to reach an understanding, Iser defines what he calls "the asymmetry between text and reader." It consists of two deviations from the norm. First, the reader is unable to test whether his/her understanding of the text is correct. And second, there is no regulative context between text and reader to establish intent; this context must be constructed by the reader from textual clues or signals.

Yet the encounter with literature has a fundamental similar-ity with other dyadic interactions in that both are concerned with an asymmetry that is corrected or overcome. Indeed, the structure of communication that Iser outlines is based on a model of imbalances being aligned or realigned through an interactive give-and-take. With the text–reader communica-tion, of course, this give-and-take has a unique character. The reader must be guided and controlled to an extent by the text, since it is unable to respond spontaneously to remarks and questions by the reader. The manner in which the text exerts control over the dialogue is thus one of the most important aspects of the communicatory process, and Iser assigns the structure of "blanks" (*Leerstellen*) this central regulatory func-tion.

Now the blank had occupied a central place in Iser's specula-tion since his "Appellstruktur" essay. There it was defined like Ingarden's "spot of indeterminacy" as the "no-man's-land of indeterminacy" between schematized views ("Indetermina-cy," p. 5). And although a good portion of this early piece is devoted to blanks and indeterminacy, what exactly constituted a blank was never made clear. One can imagine, however, that this lack of definition was intentional on Iser's part; for in response to a criticism of his undifferentiated category of indeterminacy (*Unbestimmtheit*), Iser remarked as follows: "I share the opinion that indeterminacy is an extremely undifferentiated category and is therefore at best a universal of communication theory. To define it, however, would eliminate it as a universal that determines communication."[5] The same evidently holds true for the communicative unit that governs indeterminacy, the gap or blank.

A satisfactory definition for the term in *The Act of Reading* is likewise impossible to find. Here the blank retains its centrality for communication, but in the interim it has been given a more complex function. It still is initially concerned with connecting various segments of the text. What this entails is perhaps most readily understood in considering the level of plot. In most narratives the story line will suddenly break off and continue from another perspective or in an unexpected direction. The result is a blank that the reader must complete in order to join together the unconnected segments. But this is only its most rudimentary function. The juncture of two or more segments, in turn, constitutes a "field of vision for the wandering viewpoint" (p. 197). This referential field, the minimal organizational unit in the process of comprehension, contains segments that are structurally of equal value, and their confrontation produces a tension that must be resolved by the reader's ideation. One segment must become dominant, while the others recede temporarily in importance. Iser conceives of the resolution of this tension as the filling of a blank as well, since the reader must complete an abstract framework in order to accomplish this ordering of segments.

Finally, once a determinate structure has been established, blanks appear on the level of theme and horizon.

> Wherever a segment becomes a theme, the previous one must lose its thematic relevance and be turned into a marginal, thematically vacant position, which can be and usually is occupied by the reader, so that he may focus on the new thematic segment.   (p. 198)

Because this variety of blank involves the movement of the wandering viewpoint into a thematically empty position, Iser prefers the term "vacancy" here. A blank, then, refers to "suspended connectability in the text," while vacancies designate "non-thematic segments within the referential field of the wandering viewpoint" (p. 198). The blanks and vacancies thus chart a course for reading a text by organizing the reader's participation with their structure of shifting positions. At the same time they compel the reader to complete the structure and thereby produce the aesthetic object.

The journey marked out by the blanks and vacancies remains on the syntagmatic axis in that it delineates a path "in the text." On the paradigmatic axis, on the other hand, Iser finds another important variety of blank caused by what he calls "negation." In the reading process readers will often become aware of the norms of the social system in which they live. Most literature – especially the kind valorized in Iser's theory – has the function of calling into question these norms. Through filling in blanks on the syntagmatic level the reader acquires a perspective from which previously accepted norms appear obsolete or invalid. When this occurs, a "negation" takes place, and a "dynamic blank on the paradigmatic axis of the reading process" is produced (p. 213).

Negation is an important category for Iser because it is central both to his theory of literary evaluation and to his brief remarks on literary history. Good literature, Iser implies, is characterized by the negation of specific elements and the subsequent search for a "meaning" that is unformulated, but nevertheless intended in the text. When the negation encompasses expectations or dispositions that do not transcend the reader's horizon, then the work in question is relegated to the category of "light reading." Thus the quality of the negation is a determining factor in literary value.

Here the similarities with Jauss's earlier evaluational stance towards "culinary" literature are evident, and the shortcomings of such a position need not be repeated again. Iser's brief excursion into questions of literary history entails what he calls "secondary negations." They may be defined as negations that are not "marked in the text," but rather "arise from the interaction between textual signals and the gestalten produced by the reader" (pp. 220–1). During the eighteenth century the novel appears to have included a greater number of primary negations; different perspectives in the text are continuously problematized with the switches in perspectives. In the twentieth century, by contrast, Iser detects an increase in the ratio of secondary to primary negations. The self-reflective quality of Beckett's prose, for example, is viewed as a perfect illustration of the subservience of primary to secondary negations. The total invalidation of all images constructed during the reading process has the effect of calling our attention to the very activity of communication in which we are engaged.

Negations and blanks, then, are the fundamental means by which communication takes place. They form a kind of nexus that derives from the text, but is not identical with it. In a sense one can conceive of this framework as an "unformulated double" of the "formulated text." Iser calls this double "negativity" (p. 226). As the "basic force in literary communication" negativity has three important aspects. The first is a formal feature. Unlike negations and blanks, which receive specific formulation in the text, negativity cannot be defined or precisely determined; it can only be experienced. It is like a deep structure of the text, an organizational principle whose "abstract manifestations" are the blanks and negations the reader perceives.

Negativity also plays a role on the level of content. Iser maintains that literature from Homer to the present has always contained multiple examples of misfortunes and failures: "the negativity of man's efforts and the deformation of his being" (p. 227). Deformation and failure, however, are only "surface signs" of a "hidden cause" alerting the reader to something unformulated. Since the reader has to ideate this "hidden cause," negativity has a dual function:

> Negativity is . . . at one and the same time the conditioning cause of the deformations and also their potential remedy. It translates the deformed positions into a propellant which enables the unformulated cause to become the theme of the imaginary object ideated by the reader. Thus negativity acts as a mediator between representation and reception: it initiates the constitutive acts necessary to actualize the unformulated conditions which have given rise to the deformation, and in this sense it may be called the infrastructure of the literary text. (p. 228)

Meaning in this scheme is conceived of as "the reverse side of what the text has depicted" (p. 228). It is the unformulated, because unformulatable, experience emerging from the twofold structure of negativity. Finally, from the point of view of reception, negativity is "the nonformulation of the not-yet-comprehended" (p. 229). It is the structure that enables the reader to transcend the world in order "to formulate the cause underlying the question of the world" (p. 230). In assisting us to disengage ourselves temporarily from our own lives, negativity enables us to assimilate others' views and thus is the most fundamental component of communication.

Reconciling modernism and traditionalism

The attractiveness of Iser's theory is perhaps best exemplified in his treatment of negativity. Normally seen as a destructive concept akin to decadence or nihilism, it is in Iser's hands a tool for pedagogical purposes. Negativity becomes integral to an enlightenment project long since abandoned by the tradition of "negativity" theorists, from Nietzsche and Adorno to Heidegger and Derrida. This uncanny ability to merge modernism with more traditional views is, indeed, a hallmark of Iser's work. On the one hand, the degree and quality of indeterminacy in texts are viewed as defining characteristics for literature in general. In fact, the trajectory of literary history is described in terms of an increase in indeterminacy in the "Appellstruktur" essay or, in a more sophisticated version in *The Act of Reading*, as the increase of secondary over primary negation. It may be somewhat paradoxical to see this development appraised with an organic metaphor: "In modern literature negation comes, as it were, into full flower" (p. 219). But Iser evidently sees the decisive and natural feature of literary endeavor in the framework of negation. "A fictional text," he writes, "by its very nature must call into question the validity of familiar norms" (p. 87).

But while Iser valorizes tenets more conducive to modernist poetics and European avant-garde movements, he does not completely reject more conventional functions of literature. Time and again we are reminded of the "moral" we (or the historical reader?) should draw from a given work. In *Joseph Andrews*, for example, Iser analyzes the scene in which Lady Booby attempts to seduce the hero. Recognizing the hypocrisy of her actions and comparing them with parallel scenes in the novel, the reader is called upon to reach the appropriate, enlightened conclusion: "in seeing through social pretenses, he discovers basic dispositions of human nature" (pp. 142–6). Even modern novels, whose lesson may be that there is no moral, are placed in this didactic context. In William Faulkner's *The Sound and the Fury* "the constellation of mental images provoked by the blanks" should provide us with "the key to the meaning of the novel," namely, "the senselessness of life" (p. 220). And in Samuel Beckett's prose we reach an understanding of "finiteness as the basic condition of our productivity."[6] In each case, if we read properly, we are able to grasp the appropriate lesson. Literature helps us to lead better, more productive lives, Iser intimates, even if its pedagogical method is conceived as originating in negativity. Schiller's aesthetic education has found in him a proponent capable of adapting modernist vocabulary to enlightenment ideals.

Iser is able to accomplish this uneasy union only by biasing his model towards the proclivities of his most likely readership. His theory is filled with statements that most students and teachers of literature would like to believe are true, but that lack analytical justification or empirical proof. His treatment of the reader is a case in point. For although Iser postulates a "transcendental construct," in reality his reader approximates the ideal of an educated European. Throughout *The Act of Reading* we encounter a competent and cultured reader who, contrary to Iser's wishes, *is* predetermined in both character and historical situation. This reader must be attuned to the social and literary norms of the day. In the eighteenth century he/she must have a good command of, say, Lockean philosophy, while in the twentieth century he/she should, like Iser, favor works of the traditional avant-garde. Assertions such as the following are revealing of this attitude: "The *roman à thèse* tends to bore us [?] nowadays, for it allows its reader only sufficient latitude to imagine that he is accepting voluntarily an attitude that has in fact been foisted upon him" (p. 194).

The reader promoted by Iser should also be a paradigm of "liberalism." In fact, unless he/she endeavors to rid him/herself of ideological "biases," a correct reading of the text will be precluded:

> The more committed the reader is to an ideological position, the less inclined he will be to accept the basic theme-and-horizon structure of comprehension which regulates the text–reader interaction. He will not allow his norms to become a theme, because as such they are automatically open to the critical view inherent in the virtualized positions that form the background. And if he *is* induced to participate in the events of the text, only to find that he is then supposed to adopt a negative attitude toward values he does not wish to question, the result will often be open rejection of the book and its author.   (p. 202)

Commitment to an ideological position thus impedes proper understanding. Indeed, the object of reading modern texts like Joyce's or Beckett's is to allow assimilation of "the openness of the world" into "the reader's conscious mind" (p. 211). Once again, in casting post-enlightenment literature into an enlightenment mold, Iser imbues modernism with a mainstream morality more congenial to the liberal traditions of the academy.

Consequences of phenomenology

The espousal of a liberal world view, however, does not mean that Iser purges his theory of all biases. The very proposition that prejudices are a hindrance rather than an enabling factor for understanding is, if we recall Gadamer's discussion of this topic, a debatable point. Privileging an "open" reader may reveal itself not only as a prejudice, but as an idealistic conception of social interactions as well. The line between knowledge and interest has never been drawn from a disinterested position.

But besides the "liberal" reader, Iser also depends on a certain type of text and reaction for his model. A successful work of literature, for example, must not be too obvious about the way it presents its elements; otherwise, the reader would lose interest. "If a literary text does organize its elements in too overt a manner, the chances are that we as readers will either reject the book out of boredom, or will resent the attempt to render us completely passive" (p. 87). One has the impression here and in other, similar passages that the text or author is furtively manipulating reader responses for – in Iser's benevolent system at least – therapeutic and enlightenment goals. Moreover, Iser's text functions, as we have seen, only as a negation of norms. Literature would be "barren," we are told, if we only encountered the "already familiar" (p. 43); at another point we read that the familiar territory is "interesting" only because "it is to lead in an unfamiliar direction" (p. 70); and with reference to the repertoire Iser states that fictional texts bring elements before us in unexpected combinations "so that they begin to be stripped of their validity" (p. 61). A certain version of the text and its reception is thereby validated, and it is one that most educators would probably like to believe.

But it is by no means certain that this model is appropriate either to the literature of the pre-modern period or to the typical reading experience throughout history. Nor can one concur so readily with Iser's contention that "the reader's enjoyment begins when he himself becomes productive" (p. 108). Such a remark is, within Iser's system, either a truism – because the reader is always productive – or a discriminatory comment towards forms of popular literature and culture that do not place high demands on its consumers. Again, we might feel that readers ought to enjoy only when they are productive or that literature ought to engage its readers in an active fashion, but Iser appears to use this hope, wish, or ideal illicitly in describing his allegedly phenomenological model. Like Kant's "general consensus" in the *Critique of Judgment*, Iser's model vacillates between normative presentation and utopian projection.

Iser's predicament originates in his adoption of an ahistorical, phenomenological starting-point. By conceiving the text–reader relationship in terms of constant or timeless concepts, he forecloses an integration of historical information in anything but a superficial fashion. When he then ventures to make evaluative remarks or to discuss actual texts, the consequence is often the nexus of inconsistencies described above. Iser wants to talk about literature and literary norms in historical terms, but his phenomenology gets in his way. A historical perspective cannot be attached *ex post facto* in the guise of illustrative material or mere content for the empty structure of a repertoire; it must be integrated into the very conceptual apparatus of the system. The separation of the eternal forms of text, reading, and interaction from their historical contents thus repeats a familiar scheme of idealist philosophy. Like Kant and Husserl, from whom his system ultimately derives, Iser is unable to conceive of categories themselves as the products of historical mediation.

The phenomenological foundations may also be responsible for Iser's unwitting proximity to New Criticism. Although he attempts to define his central terms in an endeavor to avoid the appearance of "formalism," his interpretive practices most often belie his claim to innovation. Since he understands the search for meaning in literature as the "external approach," he, like the New Critics, has recourse only to "the functions operating within the work" (p. 15). Even his implied reader is ultimately an immanent construct. What we wind up with is, on the one hand, a model premised on textual qualities like gaps and vacancies and, on the other hand, the response of a reader who, since Iser shuns the historical reader, is the product of an abstracted performance.

Thus we are left either with an analysis of the text in terms of its indeterminacies, or with conjectures on how an ideal reader or interpreter is affected by, reads, or analyzes the various authorial or textual strategies. Neither of these is at odds with the best traditions of Anglo-American New Criticism and close reading. Finding indeterminacy in texts, elucidating how they have been put together, whether to elicit response or not, is hardly distinguishable from activities by more traditional critics who sought ambiguity, paradox, or irony. Speculating on how the reader reacts, filling in the "gaps," as it were, involves little more than interpreting the text. Iser's project, as far as it can be translated into analyses, remains largely within the bounds of textual criticism. As Wallace Martin has observed, Iser is really an ally of those who "wish to revitalize the fundamental assumptions of the New Criticism."[7] And that his American reception has thus far exceeded that of his colleague Jauss is due in no small part to his compatibility with this familiar critical heritage.

Iser is able to cover his New Critical tracks in part by the introduction of a barrage of terms drawn from a number of different disciplines. Several critics have wondered, however, whether this terminological overload accomplishes any purpose other than short-circuiting the reader's intellectual system. It is not at all clear, for example, why concepts from speech-act theory, phenomenology, systems theory, existentialism, communication theory, and poetics are needed to establish the main points at issue. And it is far from certain that all of these terms fit together in the neat system Iser desires. After he has discussed one set of terms and has then moved on to the next, it is not always apparent how the two sets relate – or if they do not in fact overlap. How does the implied reader differ from the wandering viewpoint or the reader's role? What are the relations between repertoire and theme, or *Gestalt* and image? Moreover, many concepts appropriated from other contexts bring with them connotations inimical to a basically phenomenological undertaking. Speech-act theory, for example, assumes a human agent with a certain intention performing an utterance, while Iser is apparently unwilling to discuss directly the author's intention in producing the literary work. The result is that Iser vacillates between attributing an intention to the words independent of human agency and ascribing the intention to the traditional author. By ripping terms out of their usual contexts and forcing them to function in his "transcendental model," Iser adds an ambiguity to his terminology, making the comprehension of his theory more arduous than it need be.

Determinacy and the Fish–Iser debate

But the most serious objections to Iser's theory have revolved around the question of indeterminacy and determinacy. In a certain respect, such objections strike at the very heart of his enterprise, since the overriding issues involve the production of meaning, who or what is responsible for it, and to what extent it is limited. The two extreme positions on these questions are associated with objectivism and subjectivism. The former holds that there is only one correct and determinate meaning for each work, often identified with the author's intention, while the latter maintains that the meaning is totally the product of the mind of the individual reader. Iser tries to take a middle position on this matter by claiming that the text allows for different meanings, while restricting the possibilities. The meaning of the text is seen as constituted by the reader under the guidance of the textual instructions. Thus readers are apparently free to concretize in different fashions or to create different meanings.

But in a number of passages Iser appears to take back this freedom. At one point the meaning of the text is defined in terms of the "meeting place" of the various narrative perspectives. The reader's role is to situate him/herself in "a prestructured activity" and "to fit the diverse perspectives into a gradually evolving pattern" (p. 35). In a similar description Iser asks the reader "to grasp the pattern underlying the connections" between blanks (p. 198), thereby curtailing severely the "subjective" contribution. And in the discussion of the segment he refers to "its determinate meaning," thus suggesting that meaning belongs to the text rather than to the domain of the reader. These inconsistencies might be reconciled with Iser's stated intention by conceiving of perspectives, patterns, and segments as themselves the products of reader activity. In this case the determinacy of these constructs would not be something inherent in the text, but rather something that is already the result of the text–reader interaction. Yet even if we justify these apparent slips, it is still difficult to understand what Iser can mean when he writes about "the message" of a work (p. 81) or "the ultimate meaning of the text" (p. 98). At the very minimum one can maintain that Iser has shifted determinacy from the construction of meaning to the level of textual potential. For the "instructions for meaning production," as in Ingarden's system, are apparently considered "verifiable" on an intersubjective basis (p. 25). There is some point, therefore, in his theory where we are no longer permitted to interpret or analyze without being subject to the criterion of a single determinate element.

In Iser's most recent and most heated theoretical encounter, however, this is precisely the point under dispute. Stanley Fish's most provocative comment on Iser's theory takes up the legitimacy of the determinacy/indeterminacy distinction itself.[8] From his metacritical perspective, this separation is possible only if one can conceive of a pure text, i.e. something that can be perceived in an unmediated fashion. He argues that since every encounter with the world, whether it is labeled "reality" or "text," involves conventions of perception, indeterminacy and determinacy are irrelevant categories. There can be no indeterminacy because there is no way that a reader can place him/

herself outside of assumptions in order to be unconstrained by the possibilities built into a system of intelligibility. By the same token, determinacy is not a meaningful designation since all creation of meaning is dependent on the "subjectivity" of the reader operating within the conventions. Fish is not claiming that the analysis of a text is impossible using Iser's model; an interpretation of any work could be performed using the distinction between textual givens and the reader's contributions:

> It is just that the distinction itself is an assumption which, when it informs an act of literary description, will *produce* the phenomena it purports to describe. That is to say, every component in such an account — the determinacies or textual segments, the indeterminacies or gaps, and the adventures of the reader's "wandering viewpoint" – will be the products of an interpretive strategy that demands them, and therefore no one of those components can constitute the independent given which serves to ground the interpretive process. (p. 7)

In other words, what we see or understand is always already determined by a prior perspective or framework that enables the seeing and understanding. Iser's system, Fish implies, is built on a false foundation.

Iser's rejoinder is interesting because it clears up some possible misunderstandings in his earlier statements, even if it does not really counter the central objection.[9] In the first place Iser corrects Fish's identification of the determinate with the given and the indeterminate with the supplied. Iser draws the following distinctions: "The words of a text are given, the interpretation of the words is determinate, and the gaps between given elements and/or interpretations are the indeterminacies" (p. 83).

Second, he agrees with Fish's contention that there is no unmediated given, but maintains nevertheless that there is "something" that restricts interpretation.

> The "something" which is to be mediated exists prior to interpretation, acts as a constraint on interpretation, has repercussions on the anticipations operative in interpretation, and thus contributes to a hermeneutical process, the

result of which is both a mediated given and a reshuffling of
the initial assumptions.   (p. 84)

These two statements highlight well the differences between
Iser and Fish: while both concur on the mediated nature of all
perception, Iser clings to a control at some level by "something." At the same time it is apparent that Iser misses or does
not wish to deal with Fish's real point. Although the mistaken
identifications may detract from the accuracy of Fish's account,
they are not the heart of his argument. Fish is not taking the
Berkeleyan stance Iser ascribes to him; he is not claiming that
only what is perceived exists. He would presumably admit the
existence of words or marks on pages as well as "something"
that exists prior to interpretation. His contention, though, is
that these "givens" are meaningless – they are not even "point-
able to" as "givens" – before we endow them with meaning as
"givens."

Thus in the first statement quoted above Iser is guilty of
confusing two uses of "given": first to denote existence ("the
words of a text are given"), and then to designate the intersubjective recognizability of existing things ("the gaps between
given elements"). For elements are only given in this sense if
they are in a system in which elements can be perceived. Before
they are called "elements," they must be interpreted as such.
Similarly, Fish does not seem to challenge the assertion that
once we work within conventions, elements or "something" in a
text will exert constraints on interpretation. He maintains
rather that the very perception of constraints or the ability to
constrain is possible only because the interpreter is already
operating within a convention or under a set of assumptions.
The real question for Fish, of course – and Iser does not ask it – is
what conventions *he* is determined by in his metacritical posture. For in putting forth his argument as valid or true, Fish must
make the assumption that his statements have a special status
that somehow escapes assumptions. He thus either contradicts
his own metacritical tenets or offers a theory as "conventional"
as Iser's.

Fish's "victory" has by no means settled the dispute. If he has
emerged on top in this recent critical skirmish, then it is only
because Iser retreated to his old position instead of attacking the

enemy polemic at its weakest point. Although an impregnable position when it is granted metacritical privilege and subjected to traditional assaults, Fish's theoretical fortress collapses under its own weight once the internal contradictions at its foundations are exposed. For Iser, however, even the defeat of this foe would not relieve him of the infelicitous aspects of his treatment of determinacy. His brief discussion of the film versus the novel form can serve to highlight one further constellation of problems with this notion.

Iser notes that the difference between the filmed version of *Tom Jones* and the novel lies in the determinacy of the optic images in the former medium. This determinacy is often experienced as disappointment or impoverishment if we have read the book before seeing it on the screen. While no one would want to dispute that films operate with visual images, this comparison and evaluation are none the less noteworthy for Iser's biases in dealing with the reading process and determinacy. Besides being a terribly unsophisticated way of looking at films, which are more "textual" than Iser cares to acknowledge, this discussion indicates the primary role that the visual plays in eliminating indeterminacy. "When we imagine Tom Jones, during our reading of the novel," Iser writes, "we have to put together various facets that have been revealed to us at different times – in contrast to the film, where we always see him as a whole in every situation" (p. 138).

But do we really see Tom Jones "as a whole" just because we see an image on the screen? In what sense is he "whole"? And does the visual image actually relieve us of our productive role, then, as Iser later indicates (p. 139)? Like Ingarden, who considered the performance of a play its concretion, Iser strongly suggests here that determinacy is dependent on sense perception and that sense perception, in turn, obviates the need for ideation. Seeing is apparently believing for Iser, and the visual image thus renders us passive consumers. Fish, in other words, may not have been so wrong in his allegedly erroneous identifications after all.

But perhaps more troublesome for Iser's enterprise is the fact that here and elsewhere freedom is granted to the reader only when it doesn't really count much at all. If Tom Jones is a pound or two lighter, an inch or two taller, or if his eyes are a darker shade of blue are matters left to the reader. In these areas we are permitted to exercise a certain liberty in filling in blanks. But when it comes to the meaning of sections of the novel or the work in its entirety, Iser leaves no room for deviating from "the message." The indeterminate often seems to involve only the trivial and non-essential details; where meaning is produced, however, the reader either travels the predetermined path or misunderstands the text.

Despite various "liberal" biases and several inconsistencies in argument, Iser's significance and value should not be under-estimated. Next to Jauss, he has been the most important German theorist to appear during the past decade and a half. Moreover, his project complements Jauss's nicely. His concern for the details of interaction with texts may bring him closer to more traditional interpretive activity, but it also supplies us with a previously underexplored avenue of access to actual texts. His system helps to elucidate the complexities involved with our most basic encounter with literature: the reading process itself. In contrast to most prior theory, Iser sees this process not as a simple appropriation of words printed on a page, but as a matrix of complex experiential and intellectual activities.

Iser's merit is that he has forced us to recognize that we cannot forgo an analysis of our own involvement with a text if we are to understand what literature is about. Nor can we any longer ignore that texts are constructed to be read, that they dictate the terms of their readability, and that these terms are enabling constructs rather than dogmatic strictures. Furthermore, Iser has been more responsible than any other contemporary German critic for introducing important European theorists into the English-speaking world. Under his influence, phenomenology has been wrenched from the New Critical stranglehold of René Wellek; the Russian Formalists and Czech structuralists have also received favorable and extensive exposure in his writings. Iser has thus had a double involvement with communication. On the one hand, he has been instrumental in bringing aspects of continental theory to the attention of an English-speaking public; and, on the other, his work has sparked needed discussion of long-neglected issues.

Alternative models
and controversies

The communication model: levels of text–reader
interaction

Perhaps the most important problem surrounding reception
theory concerns its relationship to a theory of general communication, a subject that often surfaced in intellectual circles
during the years when reception theory was launched. Topics
relating to communication were most frequently addressed by
German social scientists in this period. The work of Karl-Otto
Apel, Niklas Luhmann, and Jürgen Habermas – three of the
best-known scholars in social theory – each incorporated in
some essential fashion the practices and parameters of human
interaction. Habermas's theoretical preoccupations in particular can be viewed within the framework of an emancipatory
theory of communication. From his earliest volume on the
public sphere in 1959 to his recently published *magnum opus*
entitled *Theorie des kommunikativen Handelns* (1981; Theory of
Communicative Action),[1] he has been speculating on the possibility of establishing meaningful, democratically informed dialogue in contemporary society.

Jauss and Iser

In this climate, theoretical impulses that contributed to models
of communication were especially welcome. Although social

scientists may have taken the lead, almost every field of endeavor is currently occupied with the task of placing a previously isolated discipline into a larger framework of human interaction. Indeed, reception theory itself can easily be viewed as a contribution to this widespread enterprise. It is not coincidental, for example, that both Iser and Jauss close their most cogent theoretical reflections on reception or response with sections on communication: in Iser's case with the discussion of blanks, negations, and negativity; and in Jauss's essay via an examination of *catharsis*. Reception theory, one can easily conclude, must culminate in or be subsumed by a more general theory of communication.

This is precisely the position that both Jauss and Iser have taken in subsequent theoretical statements. The former, in an interview published in *New Literary History* in 1979,[2] indicated that he sees the common denominator of such diverse critical tendencies as Prague structuralism, semiotics, and the aesthetics of reception "in the fact that they have placed problems of interhuman communication . . . in the center of their research interest" (p. 86). Responding to the objection that reception theory takes up only one side of a larger relationship, Jauss has conceded on several occasions since 1970 that the entire literary process, not just the reception of literary works, must be the ultimate object of investigation. During the interview he admits the "partiality" of his earlier work and in hindsight analyzes the development of literary studies at Constance since 1966 as a contribution to communication theory:

> Here, attempts toward a theory of literature's reception and effect, originally based upon a science of the text, were increasingly developed into a theory of literary communication which sought to do justice to the functions of production, reception, and their interaction.   (p. 86)

Indeed, Jauss situates this concern for literary communication within a general intellectual and scholarly activity in the academic community:

> To the rehabilitation of the reader, hearer, and spectator (the "recipients") in literary studies, there correspond: the opening up of text-linguistics upon a pragmatics of speech acts and

communicative situations; the elaboration of semiotics in a cultural concept of the text; the renewed questions of the subject of role and of a "lived-world" in social anthropology, of animal and environment in biology; the return of sociology of knowledge with the theories of interaction which have become active; and the disengagement from formal or expressive logic through a propadeutic or dialogical logic.   (p. 86)

The ultimate goal, although it is still far from being realized, is an interdisciplinary "general theory of communication," encompassing and constituted by all disciplines.

In observations on "The current situation of literary theory," which appeared in the same issue of *New Literary History*, Iser reaches similar conclusions about the importance of communication.[3] In surveying contemporary approaches, he finds the curious recurrence of several concepts, and he selects three of these key terms – structure, function, and communication – for a general review of critical trends. Structure is identified with a method for describing a given text and establishing its meaning. By classifying and differentiating elements in a work, structural analysis "makes possible an intersubjective and plausible description of the composition of the subject matter" (p. 9). The limitation of this method, however, is that description and taxonomy become ends in themselves. Why meaning is produced, to what ends it is used, and who is to make use of it, are not included in the structuralist enquiry. "Structuralism leaves behind a problem which cannot be satisfactorily solved even by the variants that the concept has produced. The problem is the meaning of meaning" (p. 10).

To investigate this problem one must adopt a framework that transcends structure itself and allows an examination of how meaning functions. Functional analysis, which incorporates and supersedes structural analysis, thus involves the connections between the text and its meaning, and extra-textual reality. It has to do with the contexts in which all literary texts are unavoidably situated and how these texts enter into a reciprocal relationship with their environment. But the functional approach has its limit as well. Although it is able to account for the restoration of historical experience through the reconstruction of a past world, it cannot answer the question of the continued validity of this reconstructed world and the process of reconstituting it.

To deal with this issue, Iser's notion of communication must be introduced. For this type of analysis, based on the mode of text/reader interaction, not only includes both structure and function, but also provides an answer to the question of validity. As we have seen above, Iser conceives of literary communication as a joint activity on the part of the reader and the text, acting "upon one another in a self-regulating process" (p. 15). The validity of the literary work thus consists of the experience in and derived from the reading process:

> The text's selective utilization of the reader's own faculties results in his having an aesthetic experience whose very structure enables him to obtain insight into experience acquisition; it also enables him to imagine a reality which is real as a process of experience, though it can never be real in a concrete sense.   (p. 15)

Analogous to Jauss's more universal and utopian conception, then, communication is seen here as the last stage in the development of literary theory.

Hans Ulrich Gumbrecht

Iser and Jauss, of course, were not the only theorists to recognize the implications of reception theory for communication. Indeed, in an essay of the mid-1970s, one of Jauss's most important students, Hans Ulrich Gumbrecht, even conceives the change in paradigm in terms of communication rather than effect and response.[4] Criticizing the premature proclamation of a new paradigm, he speculates that the real change will occur only as a *consequence* of the aesthetics of reception, when literary scholarship constitutes itself as a branch of the sociology of communication.

As a contribution to this development, he outlines some basic considerations for a theory of literature as social action. With reference to the production of texts the task is twofold: first Gumbrecht advocates reconstructing as accurately as possible the authorial intention, which he labels the "subjective sense of texts as activities" (p. 401). This recourse to authorial intent is not meant to imply a resurrection of superannuated, biographically oriented methods. Rather, it is necessitated by what Gumbrecht views as a fundamental inadequacy of previous theory in failing to distinguish between normative and descriptive models. While the former makes use of a standardized scheme of the literary process, the latter operates with one heuristically conceived meaning of the text. Because of its accessibility, reconstructability, historicity, and constancy, Gumbrecht opts for the author's intended meaning as the foundation for the descriptive approach.

The second part of looking at production as an activity involves factors outside any conscious authorial intent. While the "in-order-to motives" (*Um-zu-Motiven*) focus on the subjective activity of the communicative act, the "because motives" (*Weil-Motiven*) take into account "the level of historical, social structures" (p. 402). Here Gumbrecht is concerned with those historically enabling structures that legitimate subjective desires for a certain meaning or effect, or that determine in general the form and content of literary works.

Reception constitutes the reverse side of the communicatory process. Reading and understanding a literary text, like its production, are also considered social actions, and again Gumbrecht proposes a descriptive approach to complement normative procedures. Parallel to the production activity both the "in-order-to" (subjective) and "because" (social and historical) motives would be objects of investigation. But in this area Gumbrecht feels that it would be more difficult to acquire material. While certain experiments and surveys might assist in the determination of contemporary effects and responses, evidence from the past is scarce and unreliable. Furthermore, the ultimate impact of literature on "practical activity" is nearly impossible to ascertain. In this research, therefore, we must often be content with educated hypotheses based on the accumulation of the best available information.

Karlheinz Stierle

The communicatory function of literature has also been the focus for Karlheinz Stierle, another of Jauss's pupils. In contrast to Gumbrecht, however, he advocates an examination of

the formal side of the communication process. While he concedes that the study of the history of actual reception is important for interpreting and situating texts, his concerns tend
toward a "complementary formal theory of reading that derives
its specific criteria for the reception of fictional texts from the
very concept of fictionality."[5] Like Iser, then, Stierle investigates the phenomenal nature of textual communication rather
than the history of our responses to literature and their implications for present readings.

But in his most important remarks on reading, he suggests
that Iser does not go far enough. In Iser's system, as we have
seen, the formation of illusion and images was central to the
reading process. In most fiction, Stierle too would agree that
this type of mental activity is essential for the aesthetic experience, and he labels this process of illusion formation "quasi-
pragmatic," a designation that distinguishes it from the reception of non-fictional texts ("pragmatic reception"). When we
read a traditional novel, for example, both Iser and Stierle
would concur that we transcend the boundaries of the fictional
text in creating illusions in accordance with textual instructions. In Iser's model of reading, though, we remain on this level
even though images may be negated and themes may shift or
recede into the horizon.

For Stierle, on the other hand, quasi-pragmatic reading must
be supplemented by "higher forms of reception, which alone
can do justice to the specific status of fiction" (p. 83). These
higher forms entail a type of communication that is specific to
fictional texts. Stierle argues for a pseudoreferential use of
language, an application located between its usage in simple
reference and its autoreferential function. What distinguishes
narrative fiction is this pseudoreferentiality, which may be
considered autoreferentiality in the guise of referential form.
Fictional texts thus "turn out to be a variation of systemic texts,
if *systemic* denotes texts that are concerned with the conditions of
usage of their inherent terms" (p. 80). In other words, fiction is
self-reflexive, although it appears to be referential.

The higher forms of reception are concerned with exploring
fiction in its pseudoreferentiality. Understanding (*Verstehen*),
identified with the quasi-pragmatic reading, must be supplemented by cognition (*Erkennen*) or the reflexive dimension.

For "only the reflexive turning back from mimetic illusion – produced by a quasi-pragmatic reading – to fiction and its pseudoreferential articulation discloses the formal aspect of fiction" (p. 103). We might think of this double reading process, first to produce illusion and then to thematize composition itself, in Iser's terms as the activity of the reader coupled with the analysis of the literary scholar. The former reads fiction pseudo-pragmatically, while the latter has the task of explicating the very nature of the fiction that is read.

Stierle's major contribution thus far to a communication-oriented theory of literature is to be found in the essays collected in *Text als Handlung* (1975; Text as Action).[6] What unites these various pieces from the first half of the 1970s is a concern for establishing a "systematic literary scholarship" (*systematische Literaturwissenschaft*). This entails an examination of the reflexive level or reception potential of fictional texts. As aids to his theoretical enterprise Stierle most often calls upon two impulses outside of the literary sphere.

The first is speech-act theory, whose importance for him is clearly reflected in the title of his book. By utilizing the insights of Austin and Searle, Stierle seeks to overcome the sterility of a pure textual linguistics and its concomitant neglect of communication. The paradigm of performance rather than language plays a major role in "systematic literary scholarship" because it simultaneously overcomes the one-sidedness of reception theory. If the text is understood as an objectivized schema for linguistic performance, then both the production and reception of fiction can be profitably studied through textual analysis. While Gumbrecht, therefore, advocated investigating both ends of the communicatory process, Stierle favors investigating the objective structures that mediate between author and reader. Literary scholarship thus becomes for him a variant of a science of action (*Handlungswissenschaft*), with fictional texts corresponding roughly to performative utterances.

The second theory that Stierle adopts for his purposes is semiotics. Indeed, he appears to want to merge the insights of this field with those of speech-act theory. For this reason he is particularly attracted to Louis Hjelmslev, Roland Barthes, and A. J. Greimas, since he recognizes in all three an implicit concern with signs as active elements in social interaction. In Hjelmslev he values especially the distinction between the expressive plane and the content plane of semiotics; for this point of departure is more suggestive for an occupation with *parole* than with *langue*. Thus Hjelmslev brings semiotics closer to performance as opposed to the systemic and structural concerns associated with Saussure and his adherents. Barthes's attractiveness is due in large measure to his attention to how signs communicate ideology through connotative systems. Thus the "early Barthes" of *Mythologies* and *Elements of Semiology* is preferred to the "post-structuralist Barthes" of *S/Z* (pp. 131–5). Finally Greimas is important for Stierle because of his endeavor to explore structure with respect to sense or meaning (*sens*). The application of structural linguistics to social interactions, such as Stierle finds in the works of Lévi-Strauss or Greimas, thus complements his appropriation of speech-act theory. Both perspectives ultimately dovetail in the more encompassing "systematic literary scholarship," itself only a branch of general communication theory.

Stierle's application of this dual-pronged approach to specific literary problems has produced some stimulating results. His treatment of the comic situation, for example, as an action that is determined by another (*fremdbestimmte Handlung*) and seen from the perspective of a third person, leads him to some interesting and complex speculations on how comedies fit into a scheme of communicative activity. This viewpoint also enables him to account for the uneasiness in audience response to absurd theater. While older comic modes were always accompanied by the restoration of a "reasonable" condition, against which the comic moment could have an impact, the theater of the absurd questions the foundations of the genre itself by problematizing normalcy as social consensus. The consequence is an altered process of reception in which the audience is no longer permitted to have recourse to laughter as an escape and hence to the distancing associated with earlier comedy.

Equally provocative are Stierle's essays on the relationship between the exemplum and (hi)story and the use of negation in fictional texts. In the former piece he discusses the intricate connection between narrative structure and the establishment of meaning. Only the ability to tell a story, i.e. to unite moments of being in a temporal sequence, allows us to make sense out of occurrences and, ultimately, out of our own lives, which we likewise only comprehend as a narrative. The exemplum, although displaced by the advent of a historical world view in the eighteenth century, can none the less serve as a paradigm for stories; and thus its impossibility, as Stierle's reading of Montaigne demonstrates, disqualifies the possibility of all meaningful stories.

In his investigation of negation, on the other hand, Stierle examines the implications of negating images and states of affairs (*Sachverhalte*) that are only constituted in the reader's imagination. Here again he calls upon the model of double reading – he uses the terminology "syntagmatic" and "prag-matic" reading in this piece – to elucidate the complexities of reader roles we are forced to assume in confronting texts punctuated with negations. Suggestive and thought-provoking as Stierle's essays are, however, they do not constitute by any means the "systematic literary scholarship" that he heralds. His works are filled with stimulating insights, but we do not gain a sense of consistent approach. Indeed, Stierle's portrayal of Greimas's writings could just as appropriately be applied to his own:

> Greimas's writings move about in the tension-filled rela-tionship between essay and system. For the reader this means the stimulation of an extraordinary fullness of perceptive hypotheses and beginnings of models, often connected with the forced entry into entirely unusual perspectives that open new and wide horizons; but at the same time disorientation is also often the result. (p. 211)

Likewise Stierle's readers frequently will find themselves drawn into an intriguing, but labyrinthian web of speculation and analysis.

Rolf Grimminger

The attempt to utilize insights from a variety of extra-literary disciplines for the construction of communicatory models of literature was not restricted to disciples of the Constance

School. Rolf Grimminger, for example, in his frequently cited sketch of a theory of literary communication, endeavors, like Stierle, to incorporate aspects of linguistics and the philosophy of language into a model of verbal interaction.[7] He focuses his attention on the speech event (*Sprachereignis*) as the mediator of a message between two subjects. What distinguishes literary communication for him is that this speech event takes the form of a text that signals a rupture in direct interaction. The consequences of this broken line of communication are significant for the psychological processes of both author and reader. The former enters into an unusual relationship with the text, which is conceived of as an abstract partner. In reading his/her own writing the author compares the original intention with the objectified meaning and undertakes alterations based on what Grimminger labels this "one-way" or "one-sided" communication.

In an analogous fashion, the reader's encounter with a text is a "lonely psychic occurrence." Here, too, a hermeneutical process takes place in which intentions are projected and corrected during the act of reading. In both cases, however, author and reader are in some sense users of the text – at least in so far as the text consists of signs that are intersubjectively comprehensible. Belonging to neither reader nor author, these signs have to be used or deciphered by both.

Perhaps the most suggestive aspect of Grimminger's model, though, involves the social consequences he draws from this communicative activity. In contrast to instrumental theories of literary effect or even a Brechtian model of estrangement, Grimminger feels that social protest is inextricably linked with literature. As either author or reader, the participant engages in a psychic, monologic process that is removed from or even opposed to social action. But in this involvement the individual inevitably affirms "the ethos of inner freedom." Protest, at least during the history of "bourgeois poetry and philosophy," is thus characterized by this "intellectual-aesthetic resistance to social praxis." The absence of an oppositional message is unimportant: "The protest is already included in the process of communication itself, in the retreat to the ego" (p. 5).

Günter Waldmann

The political ramifications of literary communication also enter into Günter Waldmann's reflections, although he concerns himself more with the ideology of narrative structures.[8] Like other theorists in recent years, Waldmann appropriates a large battery of thought for his "communication aesthetics," from Sartre's existentialism and Husserl's phenomenology to Saussure's and Morris's linguistics. At the center of his theory, however, stands the work of two of Germany's most prominent social scientists, Niklas Luhmann and Jürgen Habermas. From Luhmann he adopts a perspective that defines the parameters for the communication of meaning (*Sinn*). For Luhmann, meaning must be understood both as a selection from various possibilities and as a simultaneous pointing to other possibilities. In other words, meaning is constituted only inside a system or within a horizon of other options, and in this capacity it serves as a means to grasp and reduce the complexity of external reality. The phenomenal world, then, is viewed through a system of meaning in which individual potentials of meaning are realized. Thus communication, contrary to the common understanding of the term, does not entail a simple conveying of information from one participant to another, but rather the actualization of meaning. Information can only be recognized as such within a system of meaning that has prior existence and encompasses both the sender and the receiver of a given message. The transference of information can occur only when the system of meaning itself is realized by both parties in an interaction.

Although Waldmann adopts this general account, he deems it incomplete and too abstract. What is missing, he contends, is the inclusion of the ideological, socially determined moment in the communication process. For this correction or supplement to Luhmann he relies on Habermas's notion of discourse. In contrast to communicative action, which describes the relationship of human beings to each other, discourse refers to the relation to the norms that determine communicative action. It is thus a form of communication in which the very activity of communication is problematized. As such, it comprises the conditions of possibility of communication, and, for Waldmann, its distortion or perversion involves the concept of ideology. In terms of communication theory, therefore, he develops the following definition:

> Ideology is that system of meaning which gives the appearance of having its normative legitimation of hegemonic forms grounded in rational discourse . . . but which simultaneously and systematically hinders every real rational discourse that would call it into question or destroy it.   (p. 33)

What Waldmann ultimately proposes, then, in investigating literary texts, is an ideologically critical method that would analyze the strategies by which rational discourse is perverted, subverted, or promoted in the communication process.

To accomplish this mission he turns to an investigation of the "textual communicative system." Like the theorists discussed above, Waldmann too relies heavily on linguistic theory, especially the "text theory" of S. J. Schmidt, who defines the text as a universal form for the transference of language into socio-communicative action. The problem with any analysis of such communicative actions, however, is that it cannot be undertaken on a concrete, pragmatic level. Individual motives and responses are either inaccessible, unreliable, or insignificant for the systematic theory Waldmann envisions. And if the author and reader are reduced to internal components of the text, then a good portion of the analysis will amount to abstract speculation on the "real" reader and author. Waldmann proposes to circumvent this dilemma by making the meaning-system (*Sinn-system*) his object of study: "The object of communicative aesthetic analysis is the structurally homologous, aesthetic meaning-system, which is the basis of individual realizations of textual communication" (p. 49).

In constructing a model of communication that will be adequate to this meaning-system, Waldmann delineates four levels on which textual communication occurs, two of which are external to the text and two of which are internal. The first level entails pragmatic communication; the real author and real reader, their intentions and expectations are included on this plane. The next level consists of the literary communication between author and reader. Here we are dealing with the author in his/her authorial role as understood by both author and reader, as well as the reader's role conceived by author and reader. The first internal communication, by contrast, is concerned with these roles as they appear in the text. The narrator of a novel, for example, or the reader addressed directly in a book, function in this capacity. Finally Waldmann defines a fictional level of communication on which characters in a text engage in communicative activity. The entire structure is summarized in the diagram on p. 120. At the very least this scheme has the advantage of neatness. Each level exhibits a symmetrical structure of communication, and the end product of each larger communication (literature, text, fictional event) feeds into the overall heading for the next communicative substructure.

At the same time, however, such a model has something artificial and alienating about it. Perhaps more telling, though, is that using such a scheme does not really guarantee that we will learn anything more about textual communication – or literature as ideology. In fact, Waldmann's sample analysis in the second half of his book seems to confirm one's worst suspicions. In using his theory to examine the short story, "A pioneer," a narrative about a war experience by the Nazi Erhard Wittek, he arrives at no startling conclusions. Most of his results were either predictable by the very genre and ideological bias of the writer, or obtainable through the application of rudimentary techniques of narrative theory. The theoretical overkill in the first half of the volume, in other words, contrasts sharply with the rather meager rewards in the second part.

But this inadequacy of theory to practice perhaps indicates the major difficulty confronted by aspiring communication theorists of literature. On the one hand we can find elaborate systems, such as Waldmann's, developed with an abundance of impulses from philosophical, sociological, and linguistic sources. But if the intricacies of the model do not even mesh effectively with the text selected by the system's architect, then we are justified in questioning the necessity for such an undertaking in the first place. On the other hand, we have Stierle's plan for a "systematic literary scholarship" that never amounts to more than a series of loosely related sketches, each designed and applied for the particular problem discussed in an individual essay. Yet with this more "haphazard" approach, even

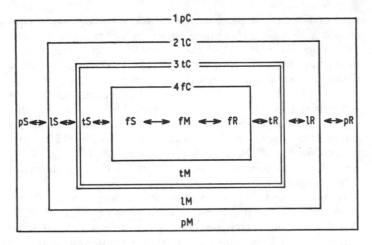

Figure 1: Basic scheme of the textual communication system
Source: Waldmann, Günter, *Kommunikationsästhetik I* (1976; p. 73)

1   pC = *pragmatic communication*
      pS = pragmatic sender: concrete *author*
      pR = pragmatic receiver: concrete *recipient*
      pM = pragmatic message: *literature* (= lC):
2   lC = *literary communication*
      lS = literary sender: author (in literary author role) as *literary*
         author
      lR = literary receiver: recipient (in literary recipient role) as
         literary recipient
      lM = literary message: *text* (= tC):
3   tC = *textinternal communication*
      tS = textinternal sender: *textinternal author (narrator) role*
      tR = textinternal receiver: *textinternal recipient (reader) role*
      tM = textinternal message: *fictional (narrative) event* (= fC):
4   fC = *fictional communication*
      fS = fictional sender: reporting *fictional (narrative) figure*
      fR = fictional receiver: receiving *fictional (narrative) figure*
      fM = fictional message: *fictional verbal and non-verbal interaction*

though it is informed by just as many outside disciplines and complicated by terminological excesses, we often witness the achievement of stimulating results. Communication theory as a framework for studying literary texts, therefore, receives a mixed review; despite some interesting possibilities, it has not yet shown itself to be the panacea for the ills of earlier scholarship. It has, however, served to remind German reception theorists bent on condemning the study of the production and description of texts to the dustbin of literary history that reception is only one aspect of a more complicated and encompassing process.

Marxist reception theory: the east–west debate

Perhaps the strongest criticism of reception theory has emanated from the Marxist camp. Although there was no lack of objections from leftists in the Federal Republic, critics from the German Democratic Republic were especially quick to point out its deficiencies as well as its contributions. When Jauss and Iser each replied to the East German evaluations, a minor debate resulted in which each side took the other to task for its "erroneous" conceptions of literary response. For GDR critics reception theory in the west was seen largely as a reaction to a crisis in bourgeois literary studies. This hypothesis was formulated in a number of important essays that appeared during the first few years of the 1970s in the GDR's central journal for literary and cultural theory, *Weimarer Beiträge*.[1] It was also repeated in a volume entitled *Gesellschaft–Literatur–Lesen: Literaturrezeption aus theoretischer Sicht* (1973; Society–Literature–Reading: Literary Reception from a Theoretical View),[2] a book that provides the East German alternative to "bourgeois" reception theory.

The authors of these views, among them noted GDR critics like Robert Weimann, Claus Träger, and Manfred Naumann, located reception theory at the end of a series of post-war methodological developments. The turn to reception, they contended, was a sign of the bankruptcy of both ahistorical formalism and bourgeois alternatives to a Marxist approach.

With this perspective on the significance of reception theory, it is perhaps understandable that the GDR's main assault has been directed against Jauss rather than Iser. For the former not only delineates more precisely the crisis of western methods; he also concerns himself more directly with the reintroduction of history into the center of literary scholarship. Iser, whose phenomenological background and inclinations could more easily be perceived in the ahistorical tradition, was at first viewed as a mere continuator of his mentor Ingarden. Jauss, on the other hand, by posing the question of reception in terms of literary history, was at once more interesting and more threatening for the GDR.

Reception and the Marxist tradition

The ambivalence with which Jauss was treated by GDR critics is probably also the result of the ambiguous role that questions of reception have played in the Marxist tradition. Two divergent perspectives on these matters can be discerned in previous Marxist criticism, and the most influential of these is indifferent, when not openly hostile, to the concern with audience response. The remarks on literature and art that can be gathered from Marx's and Engels's writings most often treat culture from the perspective of production rather than reception. Indeed, perhaps the most influential document for a Marxist view of culture, the preface to *A Contribution to the Critique of Political Economy* (1859), situates all culture in a superstructure that is determined by an economic base. When "the material productive forces of society come in conflict with the existing relations of production," a social revolution sooner or later ensues. According to a frequent interpretation of this preface, literature, as an "ideological form in which men become conscious of this conflict and fight it out,"[3] is merely a reflection or derivative of a more fundamental economic order. In other words, it is a product of social forces, not an agent of social change.

To counter this narrow interpretation of literature one could point to another passage in Marx's works that seems to encourage a concern with reception. In the "Introduction" to *Critique of Political Economy* (1857), Marx sketches some general problems in determining laws applicable to the history of culture. Using the illustrations of Greek art and the Homeric epic, he observes that accounting for the production of these cultural objects presents few problems for theory:

> The difficulty we are confronted with is not, however, that of understanding how Greek art and epic poetry are associated with certain forms of social development. The difficulty is that they still give us aesthetic pleasure and are in certain aspects regarded as a standard and unattainable ideal.[4]

Marx's rather tentative and dubious solution to this question – that we identify with ancient Greece since it is the "normal" childhood of humanity – is not really at issue here. What is important is that Marx recognized the legitimacy of questions concerning the appropriation and effect of past artistic accomplishments.

These two opposing attitudes towards reception in Marx's writings have no doubt contributed to the ambivalence of subsequent Marxist criticism. Georg Lukács and Franz Mehring, for example, seem to have played down issues of reception. Bertolt Brecht, by contrast, repeatedly stressed the importance of audience response, particularly in his theory of epic theater. Theodor Adorno considers the effect of art to be unimportant, while Walter Benjamin, especially in his later essays, devotes an increasing amount of attention to the impact of literary works. In short, the Marxist tradition provides no consensus with respect to the question of reception.

GDR criticism is thus the heir to a long heritage of ambivalence in Marxist thought on reception. Immediately following the war a traditional "descriptive" aesthetics, propagated in its crudest form by Zhdanov in the Soviet Union and with more sophistication by Lukács, became entrenched as the official doctrine in the east. Although this theory of art dominated GDR culture for at least the first two decades of its existence, other impulses were nevertheless present. Lenin's concept of the national heritage, for example, indirectly legitimized a concern with reception-oriented questions. Since many of the most celebrated works from the German past had been perverted and exploited by the Nazis, one of the most urgent tasks for the new republic was to re-examine the national tradition and purge it of its right-wing legacy. Moreover, in Germany the ideological struggle between east and west was carried over into the cultural realm in the form of a competition for claiming descent from the more progressive moments in the heritage.

The result was a sometimes excessive concern for the *Erbe* (heritage), a preoccupation that has hardly diminished over the years. This concern, however, quite naturally led to reflections on the way in which texts have a "life" quite apart from their descriptive essence. Dealing with questions of the heritage, in other words, involved an implicit acceptance of a reception-oriented problematic. This perspective was reinforced during the 1960s with the introduction of the concept of a "literary society" (*Literaturgesellschaft*). Originally used by Johannes R. Becher, the first minister of culture in the GDR, this term came to signify a co-operation and exchange among authors, critics, and the public, a communicative network that distinguishes socialist literary life from its bourgeois counterpart.

Providing a Marxist foundation

Despite the practical concern with reception in preserving the "heritage" and in forging a "literary society," it is not quite accurate to portray GDR theory as "ahead" of western criticism in this area during the 1960s. Jauss's provocation would not have been quite so provocative if GDR critics had already dealt satisfactorily with the issues he raised, and part of the initial acrimony with which his position was countered may well have stemmed from a feeling that Marxist critics should have been investigating such matters much earlier. The sharpness of response may also have been due to remnants of the "cold war of the critics"; for during the first decade and a half of the GDR's existence almost any method that even faintly resembled western theory was condemned as decadent, idealist, or imperialist.

Given this history of cold-war criticism, it is easier to understand why Jauss was taken to task particularly for his insufficient acquaintance with Marxism. In his Constance lecture he seems to derive a good deal of his knowledge of Marxist theory from dubious secondary sources, and even his revised version for his book in 1970 evidences vast oversimplifications and huge gaps. His relegation of Marxism to the positivist-historicist model of interpretation in his "Paradigm" essay of 1969 was likewise not designed to win friends in the east. As Karlheinz

Barck points out in *Gesellschaft–Literatur–Lesen*, "Jauss's premises identify Marxist literary theory short and simple with vulgar sociology" (p. 140). Those theorists who fall outside of his dogmatically conceived model of Marxist aesthetics – Benjamin or Werner Krauss, for example – are simply considered exceptions to the orthodox norm. Although some GDR critics have begrudgingly conceded that Jauss's portrayal of previous Marxist criticism has a kernel of truth in it, and although some East Germans must have welcomed the opportunity to air such criticism more openly, the way in which Marx and the Marxist tradition were handled must have seemed shabby. Jauss may not have been a continuator of anti-communism in literary theory, as one West German leftist claimed;[5] but his challenge to literary scholarship was certainly read correctly in the east as an assault on certain aspects of Marxist theory as well.

One of the central criticisms from GDR scholars, the alleged one-sidedness of the aesthetics of reception, is not unrelated to this perceived attack on a Marxist position. When Jauss was accused of "making the sphere of literary consumption absolute" (Weimann, p. 21), or at least of ignoring the dialectic between the productive and the effective sides of the literary process, the issue was not merely the insufficiency or imbalance in Jauss's model. The vehemence of the objections indicates that ideological matters were involved as well. For the proposed shift in theory from creation or description to reception can simultaneously be read as an attack on the primacy of production in Marx's general theory. Jauss's new "paradigm" could thus be seen as an implicit assault on the foundations of Marxist theory.

To defend the integrity of the Marxist position it was first imperative to review what Marx himself had to say on this matter. The relationship between production and reception had been outlined most succinctly by Marx in his "Introduction" to *Critique of Political Economy*, and accordingly the Marxist counter-model to bourgeois reception theory, undertaken by Naumann, starts with this passage. Production and consumption stand in a dialectical relationship in Marx's account. Both can be said to "produce" the other. Production "produces" consumption in three ways: by making the object for consumption, by determining the manner in which consumption takes place, and by creating a need for consumption in the consumer. "Production accordingly produces not only an object for the subject, but also a subject for the object." Consumption, in turn, defines production in two areas: it completes the production cycle and thus in a certain sense creates production, and it provides the mechanism for new production in the structuring of consumers' needs. Although these two activities thus "produce" each other, they should not be equated. According to Marx, production is the "starting-point of realisation" and, therefore, the "predominating factor" in the entire process. For consumption is conceived as "an internal factor of productive activity," and as such it is subordinate to "the act into which the entire process resolves itself in the end" (*German Ideology*, pp. 133–4).

Now the application of such a scheme to art or literature must be undertaken with great care. Facile analogies between general production and cultural production inevitably result in distortions, and Naumann seems to be aware of the dangers of a wholesale transfer from economics to art. He therefore distinguishes between the production of art (*Kunstproduktion*) and artistic production (*künstlerische Produktion*).[6] The former refers to the artist's activity as a producer of a material product, a commodity to be bought and sold on the market. The latter term designates the special activity of an artist in creating a work of art, the non-material contribution to this branch of the production process. This distinction, of course, should not suggest that one form of production has nothing to do with the other; on the contrary, these two moments are interwoven components of a single process, only separable by an abstraction from production itself. Artistic quality, however that may be defined in a given society, is manifest only in the art object, while creating art for the capitalist market will inevitably affect the form and content of art. What is important for both of these aspects of artistic activity, however, is that production is dominant. Thus, even on the level of the non-material, Naumann notes Marx's remark that the "*objet d'art* creates a public that has artistic taste and is able to enjoy beauty" (*German Ideology*, p. 133). In this model the effect and reception of art, although they are important and ultimately influence production, remain clearly in a secondary role.

Relativism and reception

The "one-sidedness" of Jauss's position can also be challenged in a different fashion. Using the more traditional scheme of basis and superstructure, the appearance of reception theory itself could be understood as simply one manifestation of a consumer-oriented society. Seen from this perspective, Jauss and others have mistaken a reflection for the essence of the problem when they valorize the consumption of art. But if Jauss has been deceived by appearances in neglecting production, then the resulting one-sidedness has, in turn, contributed to what most GDR observers regard as a deception involving the historical process. For one of the most objectionable points in Jauss's version of reception theory for eastern critics has been its tendency towards subjectivizing history.

In light of the previously mentioned criticism surrounding his demand for "objectification" of the horizon, this objection may seem odd; but here Marxists are concerned with his hermeneutically influenced conception of history rather than the remnants of inadvertent objectivism. Most often cited in this connection is the quotation Jauss takes from R. G. Collingwood: "History is nothing but the re-enactment of past thought in the historian's mind."[7] In its context this statement is used to oppose the historicist variety of historiography, but its effect, as critics like Weimann and Barck remark, is to make history completely dependent on the perceptions of the individual. By basing history solely on what is subjectively perceived, Jauss denies an objective basis for evaluating historical occurrences. Indeed, the event itself can only become eventful (*ereignishaft*) in this subjectivist scheme because it is recognized as such. Jauss, Weimann claims, has simply posited false alternatives. The choice is not between the positivistic fact-fetishism of historicism and the hermeneutical model of reception theory, but rather between false objectivity *and* subjectivity, on the one side, and "the true objectivity in historical thought" that unfolds and connects phenomena "as a process, in the reality of their movement," on the other (Weimann, pp. 21–2).

The second historical problem that results from a conception of history derived from reception concerns the alleged inclination towards relativizing literary phenomena. GDR critics have been quick to point out that Jauss's hermeneutic model, like Gadamer's, does not include any mechanism for evaluating past judgments and hence for excluding them as invalid for a consideration of the work. To take an extreme example, Nazi literary scholarship may be as much a part of the tradition as any other scholarship, but East German critics would like to have some means of disqualifying its legitimacy. According to Jauss's hermeneutical model, however, the essence of the work lies in its reception; there is apparently no metaprinciple (or objective basis) for evaluating the evaluation. All past judgments would seem to partake equally in constituting the ever-changing essence of the work. Weimann sums up this objection with the following question: "How can the literary historian historicize the norms of his pre-history without hopelessly relativizing the objectivity of the work and his own historical connection to it?" (p. 28). Behind this relativity Weimann sees Jauss making a modern virtue out of a historical necessity. For he detects a false and superficial conception of parliamentary democracy underlying such a view. And while he too would support freedom of speech or the anti-authoritarianism inherent in allowing the previously neglected views of the masses to be voiced, he does not want to purchase this superficial democracy (clothed as relativity) at the expense of the "unity of objectivity and evaluation."

Sociological failings

The most frequent criticism from the GDR, however, involves the lack of sociological grounding in the models developed by the Constance School. Barck, for example, sees the essence of Iser's theory of communication in the privatization of the reading process. Analogous to bourgeois democracy, it grants the reader a pseudo-freedom of choice, while ignoring the real societal determinants of reception.

> One can interpret it [Iser's theory of communication] as the reception-aesthetic explication of bourgeois freedom of opinion; it magnanimously allows the reader the right to constitute the meanings of literary texts, as if there were no ideology of the ruling class and no social mode of reception determined by it. (*Gesellschaft*, p. 127)

Iser's endeavor to overcome the subject–object dichotomy is thus really an avoidance of the social issues of reading. He is able to propagate a realm beyond subject and object only by valorizing reading "in its individual form" and by neglecting "its socializing function" (*Gesellschaft*, p. 128).

But once again Jauss has been the more challenging and challenged theorist in the GDR, and objections to his work for deficient sociological attention have consistently been concentrated in two interrelated areas. First, similar to the criticism of Iser, East German critics have pointed to his individualistic conception of the reader or to the normative foundations in his discussion of the reading public. As Claus Träger remarks, Jauss's reader, though perhaps active in the occupation with literary texts, does not appear to participate in making history:

> The "reader" stands so-to-speak in the air; because he is grasped *simply as a reading individual,* he is not a historical force . . . and the entire postulate of the historicity of literature as a historically constitutive force evaporates into a theory that is correct in itself, but not able to accomplish anything. (Träger, p. 21)

When Jauss has recourse to an aggregate of readers, the same insufficiency is observed. During most of the modern era several widely divergent audiences can be discerned for different types of literature, but Jauss repeatedly fails to draw distinctions on the basis of social class or origin. The public to which Jauss refers, then, like the reader, is nothing more than an idealization allowing him to circumvent decisive issues of social function. In this connection GDR critics have also faulted Jauss for his failure to account for social mediation in his model for literary history. His attempt to link literary history to general history through the concept of a socially constitutive function of literature is found to be inadequate. For the experience of the reader or the public, even if they in turn are affected by the literary work, remains contained within a literary sphere. Likewise, the horizon of expectations is conceived largely as an internal literary construct. Barck's categorization of Jauss's problem contains the essence of the GDR objection:

> For him there exists only a public in and of itself; and it is characterized merely in its quality of recipient of literature.

> Only in this quality, which finds expression in a "horizon of expectations" that is exclusively literary and not sociologically conceived, does it function as the mediator constituting the historicity of literature. (*Gesellschaft*, p. 136)

Or, as Träger summarizes, "despite all the postulates about effect, literary history, even understood in this manner as the history of reception, remains immanent" (Träger, p. 21).

Defense and counterattack

The replies of Jauss and Iser approach these objections only indirectly. Jauss concedes, for example, that reception alone cannot be used for a reconstruction of literary history; it should not be elevated to the status of an "autonomous, methodological paradigm." But this apparent concession to the criticism of one-sidedness is followed by a statement that raises the same problem in another form:

> If the historical essence of a work of art can no longer be determined for us independently from its effect, and if the tradition of works can no longer be determined independently from its reception as the history of art, then the customary aesthetics of production and description must be *founded* in an aesthetics of reception.[8] (my emphasis)

The issue, however, was precisely the ability of a reception-oriented model to deal with the relationship between production and response without distorting the artistic process.

To the objection raised by the East Germans that the unavoidable consequence of such a privileging of reception is the subjectivization and relativizing of literary history, Jauss has little to say. Instead, both he and Iser use the strategy of attacking the GDR theorists for inconsistencies and inadequacies in their own presentation. Both draw attention to an alleged contradiction between granting legitimacy to reception and still retaining a notion of reflection (*Widerspiegelung*). The mimetic function of literature, Iser claims, is irreconcilable with the pedagogical task imputed to it by GDR culture.

> When the reader is supposed to be educated to be somebody who he isn't yet, then the medium that can promote this

process cannot be the representation [*Abbildung*] of his given relations. He could only be educated when something happens to him. But to release such a happening, one needs more than the representation of real relations.[9]

Jauss notes the same contradiction and traces it back to an "idealist embarrassment" found in Marx's writings themselves. Citing the identical passage from the "Introduction" to *Critique of Political Economy* that Naumann used, he contends that Marx's notion of the artwork creating an appreciation for beauty in the public is at odds with any possible theory of reflection:

> The trouble is that the art object could hardly elicit a need that was initially quite absent in a public which the art object first has to create if beauty is to be given only the function of copying in a materialistic way. The aesthetic paradigm in Marx's dialectic of production and consumption implies that the beautiful has a transcendent ("idealist") function.[10]

And turning to Marx's comment in the *Economic-Philosophical Manuscripts* of 1844 concerning the human being's ability to produce according to the laws of beauty, Jauss finds even more ammunition for his charge of idealism:

> If the beautiful art object elicits a new and not yet existing need, it can hardly be a copy of things which are already materially present at the same time, any more than the "laws of beauty" can be drawn from that which is already materially present.   ("Embarrassment," p. 203)

Marxist critics could easily counter this last clause by asking where Jauss feels we derive our notions of beauty from if not from something that is "already materially present." But the central difficulty in both Jauss's and Iser's arguments lies in their overly mechanistic conception of reflection as "copying" material reality in an exact fashion. Not even the most dogmatic Marxist theoreticians were able to adhere to a scheme as narrow as this one, and that it is here elevated to a precept of Marxist theory, even if only for polemical purposes, seems misleading at the very least. If we understand literary reflection in a slightly more sophisticated manner – say, as an appropriation of or expansion on reality through artistic imagination – then it is difficult to see precisely where the problem lies. The contradiction here, in fact, is more readily identifiable in the attempt of western reception theorists to do away with reflection entirely from their theoretical scheme.

For reflection, despite attacks upon it from practically all philosophical and aesthetic corners in the twentieth century, has proved amazingly resistant to assault. Perhaps its biggest asset is that its opponents have to concede implicitly some legitimacy to it even while attacking it. No matter how cogent an argument one offers to disprove or discredit reflection, the argument itself could not have force without the assumption that its words and sentences – in some sense – reflect an actual state of affairs, some reality to which the words and sentences at least pretend they do not belong. Arguments against reflection, in short, are inevitably caught in self-contradiction, and Jauss's and Iser's versions are no exception. Indeed, it is difficult to imagine how literature can be socially constitutive or how it can allow us to ideate a world different from our own if all mimetic function is denied. The theories of Iser and Jauss, in other words, may not be as safe from the "contradiction" they find in Marxist reception theory as they appear to assume.

The other major theoretical point in Jauss's and Iser's response has more political overtones and involves the "freedom" accorded to the reader in constituting the meaning of the text. Both specifically point to the implications of the concept of *Rezeptionsvorgabe*, introduced in *Gesellschaft–Literatur–Lesen* to refer to the elements in a text that are "given" before interpretation takes place. The problem Jauss and Iser perceive is that this term is used to limit the possibilities of interpretation for a given work; that is, it acts as a constraint on the reader's freedom to produce meaning in the interaction with texts. Coupled with the "social modes of reception" (*gesellschaftliche Rezeptionsweisen*), which determine the reader's response through historical, social, and literary conditioning, the "givens for reception" tend to strait-jacket the reader, permitting no variety of response.

What Jauss and Iser maintain, therefore, is that GDR reception theory is propagating a conformist model of reading that effectively negates the genuine emancipatory role of literature. Since in Iser's outline of reading the therapeutically liberating function is predicated on the reader's ability to "lead another life" during the reading process, he feels that the GDR scheme, in contrast to his own, impedes the cause of freedom:

> The question is therefore to what extent a theory of reading that aims at educating to conformity with the system – however praiseworthy such a conformity may be if it is the correct one – must interfere in such processes. ... The producing of a "socialist manner of reading" demands the internalization of the correct social norms so that the subject can adapt to the society.   ("Im Lichte der Kritik," p. 339)

Jauss, too, observes a condescending and controlling force behind the East German theory, detecting "a certain mistrust as to whether the socialist reader is in fact mature enough." The role of the *Rezeptionsvorgabe*, in his view, is to eliminate indeterminacy and thus force the reader to understand the text "correctly." Although Naumann at times allows for "quite different ways" of realizing the elements "given" for reception, the reader is active only to the extent that he/she arrives at a "socialist" interpretation ("Embarrassment," p. 203–4).

Jauss and Iser are undoubtedly justified in noting the greater reliance on determinate structures in the GDR's model. They may even be correct in interpreting it as a sign of a less permissive society, although there is just as much reason to grant validity to the East German claim that bourgeois reception theory is pseudo-democratic. But when all the political invectives have been exchanged, the problem of what the text demands and what the reader supplies still remains. As we have seen in Iser's system, despite the apparent freedom accorded to an "active" reader, actual interpretations restrict the possibilities for concretization. Iser, too, implies that there is a correct way of reading the text and that its correctness is dictated by structures already present. Neither Iser, nor Jauss, nor any West German reception theorist is willing to dispense with all constraints on the production of meaning from the side of the text, and that the East Germans openly advocate principles of determinacy in their theory is more a difference of degree than of kind.

In fact, in some sense eastern critics' recourse to implicit norms of the socialist reader or to materialist views of history relieves them of the central dilemma that westerners face. Without a model of society or history, non-Marxist advocates of reception have trouble steering a course between a complete relativity and an uncritical legitimation of tradition. Indeed, the central problem we have observed with Jauss's concept of the horizon of expectations is that there is no way to "objectify" it in social or historical terms without contradicting the inherent relativizing principles he adopts from Gadamer's hermeneutics. Any statement about the structure of expectations of a past era involves judgments that are informed by theory as well as tradition. Even conceding the relative nature of any historical perspective entails assumptions about the historical process and our ability to understand it. Whether Marxist interpretations of the past are more valid or accurate than others because they claim ultimate derivation from concrete interaction with the world (praxis) is not really the problem here. What is at issue is that none of the varieties of reception theory can do without grounding in some historical presuppositions. In their responses to their GDR detractors, neither Jauss nor Iser has really faced this critical point. Thus although both sides have implicitly declared a truce in their conflict in recent years, the questions that informed the controversy are far from resolved.

Empirical reception theory: actual responses to texts

The cease-fire in the east–west debate has not meant that GDR theorists have ceased to occupy themselves with questions of response and effect. On the contrary, in practical and theoretical terms, reception studies have been as popular in the east as in the Federal Republic. Not only has *Weimarer Beiträge* in recent years carried several major essays around the topic of reception theory; the most recent theoretical volume from GDR researchers at the prestigious Akademie der Wissenschaften advocates incorporating the functional aspects of literature into the hitherto sacrosanct concept of "reflection."[1] The practicality of such a forced merger notwithstanding, such an endeavor at least indicates the seriousness with which the challenge of reception theory continues to be met in the Marxist camp.

But accompanying this attention to reception was also a

concern for delineating more precisely the sociological status of the reader. One of the most frequent ways in which this problem was approached involved studies with data gathered from surveys or other statistical sources. As early as 1970 Dietrich Sommer and Dietrich Löffler had published an essay examining the attitudes of readers towards Hermann Kant's popular novel *Die Aula* (1965; The School Auditorium).[2] Postulating a "principally possible agreement between individual and societal interests," the authors collected data concerning the needs of the reading public, its opinion of figures in the narrative, and the aspect of the novel that interested readers most. After analyzing their data, they conclude somewhat optimistically that socialist society has forged a unity between criteria of quality and effect, and they assign to *Wirkungsforschung* (research in effect or response) the task of determining these criteria. In 1978 Sommer and Löffler brought out a major study of socialist reading habits. Joined by Achim Walter and Eva Maria Scherf, they edited a volume of largely empirical investigations comprising over 500 pages and bolstered by evidence in an appendix with twelve diagrams and thirty-eight tables.[3] Included were statistics dealing with everything from traditional data on libraries and book dealers to readers' opinions on the social function of art.

The challenge to "hermeneutical" theories

The GDR, however, has had no monopoly on such empirically oriented research. In the west, during the past fifteen years, dozens of studies have appeared in which the gathering and interpretation of data, usually from the readers of literary works, have been the primary tools for the literary investigator. The reason for this turn to empirical reception theory seems to be connected with a perceived deficiency in the theories emanating from the Constance School. As we have seen above, Jauss and Iser were often taken to task for their lack of sociological grounding with respect to the reader. One of the ways to correct this failing, many felt, was to undertake analyses of the "real" reader. If this was done, it was reasoned, the abstractions of the "implied reader" or the "horizon of expectations" could be avoided.

Thus in one such endeavor Reinhold Viehoff tried to contribute to "actual reception research" by carrying out Jauss's demand to "objectify" the horizon of expectations.[4] While Jauss implied that an investigation of actual works would be adequate to the task, especially in the "ideal" cases of *Don Quixote* or *Jacques le Fataliste*, Viehoff opts for an empirical approach. Accordingly, questionnaires were sent to 106 literary critics in the Federal Republic, asking each to answer questions regarding literature "as it is" in Germany, and literature "as it should be." The specific instrument Viehoff employed in this survey was the semantic differential. The critic was given a series of adjectives and their putative opposites with a 7-point gradation between each pair. He/she was then supposed to rank actual literature and "ideal" literature on this scale. For example, critics were asked to rate literature on the spectrum from "intellectual" to "vital"; the collective results showed that actual literature was seen as "intellectual" (the rating was a 2), while it should optimally be closer to "vital" (with a ranking of 4.5). Through a battery of statistical analyses and a grouping of results, Viehoff endeavored to demonstrate the distance between the ideal and the real in the critics' literary expectations, thus making the concept of a "horizon of expectations" objective. In the process, however, Viehoff "discovered" that Jauss's category is of dubious value. The ideal construct Jauss proposes neglects the extra-aesthetic dimension, while the evidence collected indicates that this dimension determines the expectations of a significant number of critics. Similarly, the aesthetic distance Jauss had postulated as the criterion for evaluation loses its validity according to the conclusions drawn from this survey, since the horizon is shown to be too differentiated for the type of measurements Jauss suggests.

Both of these criticisms, of course, could have been and, in fact, were raised without the benefit of statistical analyses. Whether Viehoff's data provide a firmer foundation for these objections can at this point be left to the methodological preferences of the reader. For what may be more significant about empirical reception studies than the validity of its criticism of other varieties of reception theory is its self-proclaimed competition with these more hermeneutically oriented theories.

Indeed, a prolific and influential advocate of this empirical branch of reception theory, Norbert Groeben, has argued that the real change in paradigm that Jauss proclaims does not involve a shift from the immanent model of New Criticism or Formalism to the functional and effective theories of reception, but rather a change from *all* hermeneutic schemes to empirically based research. Relying on the falsification theory of Karl Popper, the analytical philosophy of Werner Stegmüller, and the notions of text-processing (*Vertextung* or *Textverarbeitung*) developed by Götz Wienold and S. J. Schmidt, Groeben advocates redirecting literary research in accord with methods already popular in the natural and social sciences.

The fundamental deficiency in previous interpretive endeavors, Groeben maintains, was the failure to distinguish rigorously between subject and object: the reader or receiver, who should be the object of literary research, was confounded with the investigator or interpreter. Since the entire communication process (sender–message–reader) is the true object of literary study, interpreting the text amounts to a confusion of the interpreter with the recipient of the message. In contrast, Groeben demands that the two should be strictly separated. Interpretation falls into the domain of the scientific investigator, who elucidates textual understanding by collecting data from recipients' concretizations. The recipient thus functions in this process solely as a medium through which the researcher can objectively observe the individual concretizations and arrive at intersubjectively valid theories. Hermeneutics, by which Groeben seems to mean all prior literary theory, is reduced to a heuristic function. Hypotheses based on non-empirical exegesis can be subjected to empirically based experimentation to establish possible validity. If a hypothesis is not proven false by a carefully controlled and systematic procedure, then it can be considered a valid statement. The techniques that Groeben mentions for conducting such experiments included many standard instruments developed by psychologists and social scientists, among them the semantic differential, free association, cloze procedure, and free card sorting.

Groeben's scheme for empirical research is conveniently summarized in the following chart (p. 138).[5] A problem is encountered by the researcher in the terminology of everyday

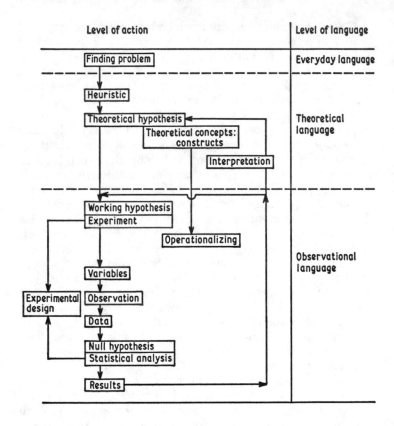

Figure 2: Flow chart of the empirical research process
Source: Groeben, Norbert, *Literaturpsychologie* (1972; p. 18)

language, and it is then reformulated in terms of the theoretical framework of the specialized discipline, in our case literary studies. At this stage a theoretical hypothesis can be stated, which is, in turn, rephrased as a working hypothesis that is subject to checks against reality, usually by experimentation involving one of the techniques mentioned above. Parallel with this reformulation, the theoretical constructs are translated into an operational model with dependent and independent variables. By adjusting the variables, researchers can observe changes and collect data. After the data have been evaluated and determined significant, the results can be used to validate or to falsify the original theoretical hypothesis. According to Groeben, this procedure is meant to ensure the most objective results possible. By continuously developing and testing hypotheses in this manner, researchers can accumulate and refine knowledge about literature as a communicative process.

The survey method

One of Groeben's earlier studies may serve as an illustration of how such empirical investigations are carried out.[6] The "everyday" problem that served as the starting-point concerned the communicability of modern lyric poetry. In reviewing the standard literature on this topic, Groeben found the tendency to categorize modern verse as hermetic or monologic, as compared with earlier verse forms. To test the validity of this general observation, he reformulated the observation in the following theoretical hypothesis: "The *communicability of modern lyric poetry* is, in its structural-aesthetic distinctiveness, *less* than the lyric poetry from the domain of *classical* aesthetics" (p. 86). To work with this hypothesis experimentally, however, it must be transformed into an operational form; in other words, it must be converted into an experimental hypothesis that can be tested. To this end Groeben connected the communicability of a text with its "value of redundancy." Communicability, Groeben postulates, increases with redundancy since the latter term implies a fulfillment of expectations or the absence of surprises. And redundancy can be measured by determining the percentage of signs that are correctly guessed by experimental subjects. Communicability can thus be grasped as a function of the predictability of signs. If we find a decrease in predictability in readers' reactions to modern poetry, then we can consider it less communicative.

To test the working hypothesis, the following experiment was devised: seventeen poems from various periods during the past 250 years were chosen at random from lyric anthologies for seventeen subjects, all students in their final year of high school. The subjects were asked to guess, in order, each sign, i.e. each letter and punctuation mark, in the first six to nine lines of each poem. After the slowest student had written down his/her guess for a given sign, the correct answer was written on the board, and the students proceeded to guess the next sign. The results of this experiment showed an average redundancy of approximately 61 per cent for classical poetry and only 53 per cent for modern verse. Groeben's conclusion is thus as follows: "In its reception by the reader *modern lyric poetry* has clearly less *communicability* than poetry from the area of *classical aesthetics*" (p. 91). The data have thus validated the initially posited significance of communicability in modern poetry:

> The circle has been closed: the results have justified both the form of the question and the manner of proceeding with which they were acquired: communicability is a central category in the structure of modern poetry; its small degree of explicitness leads to a prevalence of subjective concretization that has to be researched empirically in order to determine each given work as well as each class of poetry.   (p. 102)

From this example it should be easy to see either that empirical research methods are far from the "scientific" standard to which they aspire or that "scientific" standards are a great deal more lax than we would normally assume. Groeben's first problem occurs when he endeavors to translate communicability into terms that are quantifiable. Communication is not a simple process; it occurs on many levels and by various means. To assume that redundancy as it is defined here is an accurate measure for communication, especially when dealing with literary texts, is hardly a secure hypothesis. But even more troublesome is the way in which the conclusion is drawn. For it can easily be argued that the experiment has proven little more than that more recent poetry is *different* from older poetry. The norms of classical poetry have gradually been integrated into the very fabric of language.

Moreover, poetry itself is customarily defined against the norms of the classical canon. Thus the greater predictability of individual signs in eighteenth-century verse may very well be the consequence of socialized and internalized norms of language and poetic diction and *not* necessarily the result of a difference in communicability. To test for relative increases or decreases in communicability one would at least have to ascertain how classical poetry measured against *its* norm; that is, in a parallel fashion one would have to undertake some sort of experiment to test the reaction of eighteenth-century readers with respect to redundancy. Groeben's experiment, despite its scientific façade, raises questions where it purports to answer them, and certainly does not "clearly" prove anything about communicability.

The most general criticism of Groeben's procedure, however, is that the majority of questions that matter in literary scholarship cannot be proved by empirical methods – or if they could be "proved," they would have already been noticed by perceptive students of literature without the statistical detail. Groeben's study is a case in point. Even if we assume that communicability is indeed related to redundancy and that the procedure applied is adequate to its task, the experiment does nothing more than verify the overwhelming opinion of most observers of modern lyric poetry. To expend such a great deal of time and effort to establish the obvious seems like a colossal waste of energy and resources.

Other empirical reception studies unfortunately amount to little more than a variation on this dubious theme. Despite a variety of techniques and a great deal of statistical expertise, most contribute nothing to an understanding of the literary work and very little to knowledge about the readers of these works. A few representative examples may demonstrate why this has been so. Heinz Hillmann's experiment, reported in the essay "Reception – empirically,"[7] is perhaps most distinguished because it elicited a response from Jauss himself. His experimental procedure differs from Groeben's primarily in its openness to reader responses. Three hundred subjects were given the following text to read:

The Meeting
A man who had not see Mr K. for a long time greeted him
with the words: "You haven't changed a bit." "Oh!" said Mr
K. and paled.

The readers were not told that the text was from Brecht's *Keuner
Stories*; nor were they given any additional information. They
were simply asked to write about the text. The results were a
variety of "creative" responses in which readers filled in the
"gaps" according to personal criteria; most readers, that is,
interpreted the text with reference to their own life situation. Or,
as Hillmann writes, "the answers show clearly how extensively,
if not exclusively, the actualization is dependent on the social
group and the socialization in the school respectively" (p. 440).

But in reading this study and some of the sample "interpretations," one is apt to feel that this sort of conclusion is hardly
surprising. Indeed, Hillmann, like Groeben, seems to have
spent a great deal of time proving the commonplace, if we are
willing to grant that such spontaneous reactions constitute
evidence for something in the first place. What is worse, such a
study not only shows us very little about the readers' relationship to the text as a *literary* text, but also does not really begin
to come to terms with the apparent prejudices of the readers.
This investigation, in short, only confirms for us that one can
elicit a plethora of poorly conceived, often absurdly naïve,
responses to a given text when it is torn from its context and
used merely as a stimulus for vaguely solicited, subjective
reactions.

Werner Faulstich fares only somewhat better by using the
survey as an instrument for empirical research. In two of the five
studies included in *Domänen der Rezeptionsanalyse* (1977; Domains
of Reception Analysis) Faulstich composed detailed questionnaires and sent them to professors of English literature and
lawyers respectively.[8] Included in the first survey were questions concerning individual interests, working habits, and attitudes towards the discipline, as well as requests for personal
information. The second survey dealt primarily with reading
habits for what Faulstich considers a relatively homogeneous
group of professionals. The working hypothesis for this latter
study provides another example of empirical techniques used to
confirm what is already expected:

The fundamental hypothesis in working out the questionnaire was that a reader is not simply free in the choice of his
reading material, but rather that his preferences are determined by his needs, which in turn are largely dependent on the
experiences of primary and secondary socialization.   (p. 70)

The only question most people would have about this
hypothesis is why it needs to be proven. More questionable than
the hypothesis, however, is the method for proving it. The
techniques used for measuring such factors as needs or
socialization are often so interrelated with reading habits that
one suspects the conclusion has already been included in the
composition of the questions. As in so many empirical studies,
the instrument seems designed to evoke the appropriate response.

This manipulation of statistical techniques is perhaps most
evident in the conclusion to the first survey, which purportedly
"proves" the necessity for conducting literary scholarship with
empirical studies. Here Faulstich observes first a lack of coherence in English teachers' self-understanding as literary scholars. The problem, he maintains, is that, according to the data,
they assign literary scholarship (*Literaturwissenschaft*) the same
role as literary criticism (*Literaturkritik*). "Factually," however,
"the demands and functions of the discipline of literary scholarship are different from literary criticism; they must be clearly
separated" (p. 66). The way to do this, of course, is to define
literary criticism as an activity that operates hermeneutically,
while literary scholarship analyzes "objectively" the hermeneutical process itself. Thus "the recourse to empiricism is
unavoidable" (p. 67). Faulstich's "objective" method has thus
managed not only to detect the malaise of his colleagues, but
also to present itself as the panacea for their ills.

The statistical overkill characteristic of so many empirical
studies is best exemplified by the book-length investigation of a
single lyric poem by Paul Celan. In *Text und Rezeption* (1972;
Text and Reception) a team of six researchers performed an
extensive analysis of responses to a questionnaire about
"Fadensonnen".[9]

FADENSONNEN
über der grauschwarzen Ödnis.

Ein baum-
hoher Gedanke
greift sich den Lichtton: es sind
noch Lieder zu singen jenseits
der Menschen.

(Thread suns / over grey-black wilderness. / A tree- / high
thought / tunes in to light's pitch: there are / still songs to be
sung on the other side / of mankind.)[10]

The subjects of this experiment were drawn from students in
various elementary schools, high schools (including evening
school), and university classes; the ages of the participants
varied from 14 years to 74 years, although most fell between 17
and 24. They were asked to respond to a rather lengthy questionnaire that incorporated a variety of empirical techniques.
On the one hand, the survey included standard yes-and-no and
multiple-choice questions; on the other hand, several questions
were designed according to principles of free association and the
semantic differential.

In contrast to the studies previously examined, this experiment dealt chiefly with responses to the poem: the focus was on
readers' associations with difficult and central words like *Fadensonnen* or *Lichtton*. In addition, a certain pedagogical "manipulation" was built into the sequence of the survey. Starting with
general questions about the structure and meaning of the text,
the reader was then forced to confront the individual elements of
imagery through the semantic differential and free association
before again answering questions about the poem as a whole.
Most readers, it appears, actually came to a better understanding of what the poem meant through this procedure. In
this study, therefore, the researchers not only learned something about the readers' responses, but the readers also gained
insight into the literary work.

But it is still debatable whether such pedagogical gains are
worth the extensive statistical effort. Training individuals to
read poetry with more attentiveness to detail and more sensitivity to nuance can be achieved more effectively by other didactic
techniques. And the results of this survey, discussed in over 150
pages of text, charts, and data, bring too little of educational or
hermeneutical value to justify such an undertaking. An essay by

a perceptive critic would undoubtedly tell us more about Celan's poem than the congeries of statistics one is forced to plough through. After reading such a study, then, one is again left with the same major questions about "empirical" methods: do such techniques really prove what they set out to show, and, even if they do provide evidence for hypotheses, couldn't the same conclusions be obtained more simply and just as convincingly by other means?

The use and abuse of empiricism

Because of the limited value of most previous empirical reception research, communication between "hermeneutical" reception theorists and empiricists has been extremely infrequent. Neither "school" of research has managed to engage the other in extensive debate or dialogue, and neither takes note of the most recent work from the other's camp. If there is any agreement between the two positions, then it is probably that the tenets supporting the adversary branch of reception theory are so false that no productive relationship is possible. The empirical school, as we have seen, ascribes only heuristic value to their hermeneutical counterpart, while Jauss *et al.* would undoubtedly see the empirical method as a vestige of a superannuated scientism. Some common ground between the two, however, deserves exploration. Although the results thus far have often been tedious and disappointing, empiricism itself is not totally without a place in future research projects. Indeed, if we conceive of empiricism as, at root, an epistemological theory that defines our acquisition of knowledge in terms of experience or sense impressions, then it is difficult to see how we could avoid some recourse to it. The very act of reading a text entails sensory input of some sort. What merits extreme scepticism is not the philosophical point of departure, but its abuse when transformed into a dogmatic method claiming exclusive access to truth.

The problem with what has hitherto gone under the label of empirical reception theory is thus not so much empiricism, which cannot be avoided, as naïve scientism, which has contributed nothing to literary theory and practice besides reams of printed pages. If empirical research in the future is to play a useful role in larger critical projects involving response and effect, it will have to assume a more modest and ancillary function. Studying actual readings of a given text can be and has been a beneficial undertaking for exploring the dynamics of the text and the sociology of the reader. Looking at the composition and habits of different readerships can supply information that helps clarify the entire literary process. Even experimental methods, when employed with extreme caution, can provide insights into the way in which reading occurs – a subject about which very little is known. Continuing on its present course, empirical reception theory is bound to remain an isolated and ridiculed branch of literary endeavor. Purged of its absolutist notions about objectivity and applied in a judicious manner, on the other hand, empirical studies could become a boon rather than a bane for our understanding of the literary text and its reception.

5
Problems and perspectives

The popularity of empirical research in reception studies since the mid-1970s may be the symptom of a more general crisis in reception theory. Based on the experimental methods of the natural sciences, empirical investigations have thus far represented a retreat from the hermeneutical and phenomenological points of departure; or they have understood themselves as mere suppliers of data and results for more encompassing models of literature. In no case, however, have they been able to provide advances on the literary theory of the Constance School. On the theoretical front, though, the most noted advocates of non-empirical methods have been equally unproductive during the past few years. The last major works by Stierle and Iser appeared in 1975 and 1976 respectively, and although a revised and expanded edition of Jauss's *Aesthetic Experience* has recently been published in Germany, it does not appear to offer any major theoretical breakthrough.[1]

The apparent stagnation in reception theory is not necessarily an indication of intellectual bankruptcy, though. It can also be seen as evidence for the fecundity of the initial speculative activity, since proponents have now settled into more detailed and well-defined areas of research. Using the terminology of Kuhn's model, one could conceive of the last five to ten years as a period of "normal science" in which no major "revolutions" have occurred to disturb the dominant paradigm.

Yet one can also view the dearth of new theory as the consequence of various impasses that have been reached when the original hypotheses of reception theory were logically extended. Reception theory has undoubtedly had a tremendous impact on the way in which literary studies are now conducted, but the paths it has explored have not always proved to be as open and productive as originally envisioned. Detours, dead ends, and circular trails have been frequently traveled. These become apparent when reception theory is confronted with the variety of positions associated with structuralist, poststructuralist, or other "avant-garde" directions in France and in the United States. For in these theories we likewise encounter a proliferation of discourses that challenge the dominant way of thinking about literature – and frequently in a more radical, if not always a more productive, fashion. In concluding this introduction to reception theory, therefore, it is perhaps most appropriate here to examine briefly four areas (text, reader, interpretation, and literary history) in which the ramifications as well as the limitations of this reorientation of scholarship have been most evident, and in so doing to touch upon some of the differences between reception theory and other trends in contemporary criticism.

The stability of the text

Let us begin with the seemingly simple notion of the literary text. Before the advent of reception theory, the text, usually understood as the verbal work of art or the literary artwork, reigned supreme. Influenced by Anglo-American New Criticism and drawing on a native tradition of stylistic analysis, German scholarship in the early post-war period directed attention to close reading or explication of texts. Reception theory undermined such interpretive practice by viewing the text as a function of its readers and its reception. The conception of an objective and eternal work of art with a unique structure and a single, determinate meaning was replaced by a variety of models in which the essence of the work is a never-completed unfolding of its effective history, while its meaning is constituted by the interaction between text and reader.

In Jauss's aesthetics of reception, for example, the text that we read is never separable from its history of reception. The horizon in which it first appeared is both different from our own and a part of our own in that it is temporally distant from, yet constitutive of the present horizon. The text as a mediator between horizons is consequently an unstable commodity: as our present horizon changes, the nature of the fusion of horizons alters as well. Thus the understanding of the text, which is made possible by this fusion, becomes a function of history. In short, the text is grasped in its becoming rather than as a fixed entity.

Iser introduces a different set of considerations that are just as destabilizing for the traditional view of the text. For him the artwork is constituted by and in the act of reading. The essence and meaning of a literary work do not belong to the text, but to the process in which textual structures and the reader's ideation interact. During this interaction the reader is assigned the task of constructing a hitherto unformulated and unique work of art and of discerning patterns of significance that arise from these constructions. The reader's activity in generating meaning, not the allegedly inherent message of the text, is the focus of Iser's concerns. From varying perspectives, therefore, both Jauss and Iser dismantle the older construct of the text as the stable foundation of interpretation and literary history. Displaced from the center of literary study, the text in reception theory lives only through the reader and the history of the reader's involvement with it.

Still, one can argue that the displacement Jauss and Iser advocate represents only an apparent shift in interpretive focus. Despite the rhetoric of "readers' rights," the text as a stable and determinate structure often manages to intrude into the very heart of reception theory. Jauss's dependence on an objectification of the horizon of expectations or his endeavor to describe a work in terms of textual linguistics are two cases in which we have already detected a furtive reintroduction of textual determinacy. In order to reconstruct past literary horizons we must assume the stability of the texts that constitute these horizons. Similarly, the linguistic signals Jauss finds in texts recall an earlier paradigm of interpretation in which a supposedly neutral observer described the literary work as a constant structure. Iser's discussion of textual determinacy, which has likewise been registered in chapter 3, may also be seen as a maneuver which gives new stability to the text. Even if the work of art is granted indeterminacy, the underlying structure that enables the variety of readings remains constant in his theory.

At some level, both Iser and Jauss, as well as other reception theorists, call upon a determinate text (or sub-text) to prevent what threatens to be a totally subjective and arbitrary reader response. Within a conventional framework, of course, there is nothing wrong with proposing that the text is determinate. In a model based on reception or effect, however, it raises two problems.

First, it potentially undermines the novelty and consistency of the approach. If we ultimately have recourse to features of a knowable text, then the suspicion can easily arise that reception theory has frequently changed only the critical vocabulary, not the way in which we analyze literature. Instead of the "spirit of the age," we find the "objectified horizon"; in lieu of the ambiguity and irony in the text, we read about gaps and indeterminacies. But even if we grant a partial shift in focus, the problem of establishing the determinate portion of the text still remains. If the essence of a text is in its becoming, how are we to describe it in anything more than a provisional fashion using "signals"? And what allows us to permit variability in what a reader ideates, while simultaneously denying it in elements that, according to the literary scholar, belong to the inter-subjectively verifiable enabling structure? By destabilizing the text and surreptitiously introducing aspects of textual deter-minacy, reception theorists appear to have painted themselves into a theoretical corner. The tools that they can utilize for textual analysis should be unavailable to them if they are consistently "receptive" or "effective." If these tools are none the less introduced, they can be accused of merely displacing determinacy from one textual level to another.

The disappearing text: Stanley Fish

It is possible to be consistently "anti-textual," of course, but this theoretical postulate provides only a secure position for argument. In practice we have to pretend that the text exists and that we can make statements about it. The work of Stanley Fish is perhaps the best illustration of such a theoretical antitextualism combined with a practice of rigorous attention to textual detail.[1] In his theory Fish shifts the onus of interpretation squarely on to the reader. For him there are no textual signals or intersubjective structures outside of conventions that an interpretive community has already agreed upon.

In this sense one could say that the text contributes nothing to interpretation; everything is dependent on what the reader brings to it. To the questions: what does the reader then read? or what does the critic interpret? Fish has no answer. But he feels that no one else could answer these questions either, since any attempt to establish an objective essence independent of the reader, even if it were only black marks on a white page, would already be made from a position inside of an interpretive community. The text, in short, disappears at this metacritical level because Fish considers any statement about it to be informed by prior conventions of interpretation (in the broadest sense of the word).

However, in his interpretive encounters with texts – or whatever he feels he encounters in reading – Fish most often devotes himself to a minutely detailed account of the generation of meaning and paradoxes. This practice is not at odds with his theoretical positional because Fish claims no greater validity for his reading than for any other. If we agree with his interpretation, it is because we have adopted his conventions. His work is not more correct than others', it is at most more "interesting."

But this solution to the nasty perseverance of textual determinacy is ultimately unsatisfactory. To accept Fish's position we must accept all of his metacritical assumptions about conventions and communities. As we observed before, though, Fish's own position is by no means immune from his own metacriticism. Why shouldn't Fish's statements also be already determined by an interpretive community and thus be subject to the same suspended validity as others'? Furthermore, even if we could accept Fish's position, he has accomplished little more than a shift in determinacy from the text to another construct, whether it be called reader, convention or community. The apparent stability of views on some texts or on the fact that texts are stable may be the consequence of membership in a cohesive interpretive coterie, but where does this group's stability originate, and how can it be defined and determined? The text may indeed disappear in Fish's model, but determinacy simply crops up in another guise. Even if we agree that nothing belongs to the text, that it is ultimately not describable, as soon as we register similarity of interpretation, we are bound to admit something determinate, controlling our agreement in interpretation.

The rise of the reader

Reception theorists have tended to call this controlling force the reader, and much of their work can be understood as an attempt to demonstrate how the reader is the ultimate source of meaning and literary history. Despite occasional lapses into textual objectivism, the rehabilitation of the reader must be taken seriously. In recent years there has been no topic more hotly debated on the German scene. Most of the controversy thus far has focused on what reader-oriented research entails. Empirically based studies have insisted on looking at actual people reading texts, while hermeneutical and phenomenological models have usually opted for some variety of heuristic construct, and this basic split – and the attempt to overcome it – has fueled much of the discussion.

But even within these two large groupings there is apt to be a great deal of disagreement on matters of detail. Erwin Wolff, for example, concurs with Iser concerning the necessity for developing a non-empirical category, yet disagrees with him on the precise constitution of the reader and the manner to determine his/her role. In contrast to Iser's implied reader, Wolff suggests an "intended reader," that is, one that the author has in mind for his/her work.[1] In most cases this construct will overlap with Iser's, but it is not completely identical. For Wolff's reader is more a creature of literary history than of pure reading – although such a distinction can never be drawn with exactitude. The intended reader can be determined not only by textual clues in the work being read, but also by adjacent works and even by the author's (and presumably other authors') remarks on his/her public.

What interests Wolff, therefore, is the idea of the reader in its historical unfolding. Iser, on the other hand, is only concerned with the reader who is competent to interact successfully with a specific text. His reader is thus always performing and is inconceivable apart from the "act of reading," while Wolff's can be posited as an ideal type, independent from any one text. The point here, however, is not which reader is more useful or appropriate, but rather that recent theory has occupied itself with such minute distinctions, producing a seemingly endless stream of increasingly "refined" reader concepts, which differ from each other only by nuances. Wolff himself, for example, mentions an imaginary reader, an appropriate reader, an ideal reader, an idealized reader, and an immanent reader in his essay. Looking outside Germany, we could easily extend this list with Riffaterre's superreader, Fish's informed reader, or Prince's narratee. Despite their differences, what seems to unite all of these constructs is their function as a lightning rod with respect to the "work itself." The addressee, consumer, or recipient is no longer seen as a marginal element in literary studies. Particularly in the German models, the reader has become, in Jauss's words, the "arbiter [*Instanz*] of a new history of literature."[2]

The decentered reader: Roland Barthes

If we measure the fruitfulness of an approach by the amount of research and theoretical discussion it has generated, then the shift to examining the reader, whether understood as historical person or heuristic construct, has been an enormous success. Indeed, the novelty and attractiveness of reception theory is no doubt inextricably linked to the flexibility built into a reader-oriented model. At the same time, though, this orientation entails limitations that "avant-garde" theorists in France or the United States would associate with much of contemporary German criticism.

The recourse to a reader almost inevitably involves a centering of critical focus on a human subject. This subject is then confronted with an object called the literary text, which is supposed to be read or interpreted in the reading process. As both a historical entity and a textual function, the reliance on a reader thus introduces the very subject–object dichotomy that has been recently decried for its metaphysical foundation.

In contrast to the decentered notions of the subject so fashionable in post-structuralist circles, reception theory harks back to a conventional framework of interpretive endeavor. Rather than announcing the death of the human being – the calling card of French theorists from Foucault to Lacan – German criticism, despite its radical posturing, seems to be refurbishing the much maligned "humanist" tradition. To appreciate the "conservative" nature of reception theory *vis-à-vis* post-structuralist models, we need only compare Roland Barthes's notion of the reader in S/Z^1 with the variety of readers that most often crop up in reception theory.

Barthes problematizes the common notions of reading in his reflection on the seemingly simple sentence: "I read the text." Like reception theorists, he grants the "subject" a productive role in the reading process: "The more plural the text, the less it is written before I read it." But unlike the German critics, he extends this plurality to the "I" as well; consequently the reading process itself changes. It is no longer conceived as just another example of a defined subject performing an action on a knowable and pre-existing object:

> I do not make it [the text] undergo a predicative operation, consequent upon its being, an operation known as *reading*, and *I* is not an innocent subject, anterior to the text, one which will subsequently deal with the text as it would an object to dismantle or a site to occupy.

What distinguishes Barthes's "reader" from those encountered in reception theory is that his is composed of an infinite number of codes or texts. It is not a unified center from which meaning and interpretation originate, but rather a construct characterized by dispersion and plurality: "This 'I' which approaches the text is already itself a plurality of other texts, of codes which are infinite or, more precisely, lost (whose origin is lost)." If we assume that Barthes is here espousing what would approximately correspond to a "post-structuralist reader," then the differences between German and French criticism can be easily summarized: while reception theorists have displaced their interpretive focus from the text to the reader, post-structuralists have displaced all focus by textualizing the reader.

Interpretation and the search for meaning

A similar distinction can be drawn if we examine current notions of interpretation. Once again reception theory takes a position that is apparently opposed to traditional practices, but not very radical from a variety of current perspectives. The oppositional posture can be most readily observed in Jauss's adoption of Kuhn's paradigm model. As we have witnessed earlier, the application of the notion of a scientific revolution to literary studies can be evaluated as an attempt to separate the interpretive thrust of reception theory from older, obsolete hermeneutic endeavors. In fact, one of the central concerns for the new paradigm is that it be able to provide new interpretations of older works, thus rescuing and rejuvenating the literary canon.

Interpretation, then, conceived as the activity of a reader in understanding a text, remains a focus of Jauss's theory. The same holds true for Iser, whose thoughts on this issue occupy the entire first chapter of *The Act of Reading*.[1] Here he argues strongly against the "form of interpretation which is concerned first and foremost with the meaning of a literary work" (p. 3). More specifically he opposes the "referential model," in which the reader is called upon to hunt for a truth tucked away in the folds of the textual fabric. Twentieth-century criticism, although it has sought to escape from this "classical norm of interpretation," has inevitably wound up capitulating to it. Iser's primary example of this is New Criticism. Rejecting the view of a work as "an object containing the hidden meaning of a prevailing truth," this Anglo-American school preferred to concentrate on "the elements of the work and their interaction" (p. 15). By refusing to play the meaning game, these critics avoided the pitfalls of earlier exegetic enterprises – but not entirely. For in their recourse to harmony and the removal of ambiguities, Iser claims that the New Critics reveal their adherence to the "old values."

Iser's alternative, which has been outlined in greater detail above, involves paying more attention to the process than the result. Meaning for him is not to be dug out of the text or pieced together from textual clues, but rather is reached by an interactive process between reader and text. Likewise, interpretation does not entail the discovery of a determinate meaning in the text, but the experiencing of the work as this process unfolds. Whether Iser actually adheres to this model in his practice is not the point here. What is at issue is the putative opposition of reception theory to conventional practices. Both Jauss and Iser present their approaches as a break from the accepted ways in which texts have been previously analyzed.

And from a certain vantage point, of course, reception theory *does* break with older notions of interpretation. With the reader at the center of the interpretive project, it was possible to generate an evolutionary model of literary history as well as an interactive theory of reading. But we should wonder, none the less, whether this refocusing of critical activity does not itself retain more of the "old values" than reception theorists recognize. As we have already noted, the most general tendency of reception theory has entailed the shift of attention from the text to the reader. The determinate text to which traditional criticism had adhered was thus supplanted by the recipient. There is no reason to believe, however, that the consumer of literature is any more stable than the volatile text. Even if we do not accept Barthes's textualization of the reader, why should we be able to read the reading subject or this subject's reading more easily or accurately than what the subject was reading? In the face of textual ambiguity, the displacement of critical focus from the text to the reader retains the determinacy of the critical heritage by relocating it. We admit that the text is multiple while simultaneously denying the plurality of readers and their writing.

Indeed, reception theorists share this critical strategy and its limitations with the two most popular varieties of reader-response criticism in the United States. Jonathan Culler's desire to establish a "structuralist poetics" and Fish's frequent references to literary communities and their attendant conventions are plagued with analogous problems in that they both appear to suggest some realm in which the indeterminacy of the interpretive enterprise is halted by a readable and determinate agency.

For Culler the difficulty arises when he writes of literary "competence" and endeavors to elucidate the "set of conventions for reading literary texts" that inform this competence.[2]

While he is undoubtedly correct in assuming that rules and conventions allow us to make sense out of literature, any attempt to formulate these enabling rules will inevitably encounter the same problems that led critics to abandon the notion of a determinate text. Why should we be able to pin down conventions – which are, after all, abstracted from texts – if the texts themselves remain always elusive? Or, to state the problem differently, why shouldn't the conventions be infinitely extendable, like interpretations of texts? And why shouldn't we be able to find another, larger controlling agency (e.g. society or history) that oversees the conventions and is thus a more appropriate object for study?

Fish produces a similar dilemma in his metacritical polemics when he refers to literary communities, and perhaps it is not insignificant that his introduction of this term involves an obvious circular argument: literary communities exist because of observed agreement among critics, and agreement exists because of common membership in a literary community. That Fish seems unwilling to fight his way out of this circle by suggesting other criteria for his communities suggests that he may be aware of the theoretical tangle in which he is ensnared. When such strategies are used as a substitute for conventional interpretation or to facilitate access to the text, the question that may be posed is why should we be able to read the reader, the convention, or the institution any better than we can read the text?

The necessity of misinterpretation: Harold Bloom

To admit that one would encounter difficulties with determinacy in researching the reader, conventions, or the institution of art does not mean, of course, that such activities are not useful. The argument here is rather that investigating these areas involves the same kinds of problem that one meets in looking at the literary text. Trying to circumvent the text by displacing the critical focus on to another agency only amounts to a postponement of the confrontation with determinacy.

A total avoidance of this issue can only be achieved if interpretation itself is cast in a different framework. And this rethinking of interpretation is precisely what separates a "postmodernist" perspective from models that depend on reader response. Reception theorists, in dealing with interpretation, reinforce a model in which a subject produces a written or oral statement that explains or provides the meaning of a primary text. The interpretation is thus considered derivative, parasitic, or marginal. Its own textual qualities are of secondary importance since it purports to explain in plain, discursive prose what has been composed in a figurative, literary language. "Postmodernist" critics, by contrast, deny this commonly accepted relationship between text and commentary. Criticism in this frame of reference does not involve an interpretive act as much as a creative one. The emphasis here is not on the secondary aspect of interpretation, but rather on the production of new texts. In spatial imagery one could say that commenting on a piece of literature entails adding a layer on top of or even next to the text, as opposed to penetrating into or coming closer to something primary.

Although most post-structuralists share this view of critical activity, perhaps the strongest statement of this position comes from Harold Bloom. His conception of reading demonstrates once again the problems that reception theory faces in gaining acceptance in "avant-garde" literary circles. Most of Bloom's interest is directed at how poets read other poets. His central thesis, that each strong poet necessarily misreads his/her great precursor, is meant to provide a general theory of poetic influence. But his notion of reading also has implications for the critics' or scholars' activity.

Misinterpretation – or, to use Bloom's own vocabulary, "misprision" – is viewed as the constitutive act of reading, interpretation, and literary history. It is never possible to restate a poem or to come "closer" to its meaning, as a conventional critic might believe. The best we can do is to compose another poem, and even this reformulation is always a misinterpretation of a parent poem. What distinguishes poems from what we normally call criticism or interpretation is thus only that the former misprisions are customarily more extreme than the latter:

Poets' misinterpretations of poems are more drastic than critics' misinterpretations or criticism, but this is only a difference in degree and not at all in kind. There are no interpretations but only misinterpretations, and so all criticism is prose poetry.[1]

Criticism is conceived here as "a series of swerves after unique acts of creative misunderstanding" (p. 93), while the best interpretations, recast as misinterpretation and prose poetry, consist of the most imaginative and "antithetical" texts in the guise of commentary.

Reconstituting literary history

With such a notion of interpretation, it is not surprising that reception theory should differ considerably from "avant-garde" criticism with respect to literary history. Once again, the German contingent cannot be charged with a total lack of innovation. Especially in its earliest phases, as exemplified in Jauss's writings, reception theory concerned itself with rethinking the relationship between literary history and interpretation, on the one hand, and literary history and general history, on the other. An interpretation of a text could no longer be undertaken by simply placing it in its historical context; rather, the history of its very interpretation was considered an integral part of our ability to understand it. Literary history, then, could not be the positivistic chronicling of authors and movements; based on an evolutionary model, it had to emphasize the eventful (ereignishafte) nature of the literary work as well as its constitutive historical role.

One of the most important consequences of such a redefinition of literary history was the hypothesis of a reversal in the relationship between the history of cultural phenomena (art, literature, music, etc.) and pragmatic history (Historie). Formerly each branch of cultural history was considered to be a derivative of the more encompassing historical process; culture, understood as epiphenomena, was a realm dependent upon a political, economic, or societal base. But Jauss's early project can be read as an endeavor to overturn this sort of model. A history of art based on an aesthetics of reception would compel us to rethink the notion of pragmatic history: "The history of art, through its continuous mediation of past and present art, can become a paradigm for a history that is to show 'the development of this present.'"[1] What Jauss is opposing here is the tradition of nineteenth-century historical objectivism, which claimed the existence of objective facts independent of the observing subject. The aesthetics of reception, by relativizing all facticity with its proposition of a dialogue between past and present, supplies an alternative model for comprehending past occurrences. The recruitment of art as a paradigm for general history would thus mean the elimination of "the substantialist idea of tradition" in favor of a "functional idea of history."

History as metaphysics: Jacques Derrida

Some of the drawbacks to such a notion of history have been noted already when the East German objections were registered. The challenge of the "avant-garde," however, is of a different nature. Not just the way in which we approach an understanding of the past, but the very notion of historical thinking is here called into question. In the same year that Jauss delivered his manifesto of reception theory at Constance, Jacques Derrida, for example, published a volume that seemed to call for the annihilation of history itself.[1] Although he occasionally alludes to what appears to be a traditional conception of history – e.g. in his call for a "history" of the contrast between natural writing and artificial inscription (p. 15) – his project in *Of Grammatology* has often been viewed as an endeavor to break from all conventions of historical thought. In analyzing Rousseau's text *On the Origin of Languages*, he demands that

> reading should free itself, at least in its axis, from the classical categories of history – not only the categories of the history of ideas and the history of literature but also, and perhaps above all, from the categories of the history of philosophy.
>
> (p. lxxxix)

Indeed, his very procedure in *Of Grammatology* – moving from a consideration of Saussure "backward" to an in-depth study of Rousseau, sprinkling in various other writers from the history of philosophy along the way – testifies to his indifference to discussing his central themes in any conventional chronological sequence.

But his most serious objection to history as it has been

conceived and practiced by previous generations is that it too belongs to the metaphysical system that he is determined to deconstruct. "The concept of history itself," he writes in his "Exergue," only has meaning "within a logocentric epoch" (p. 4). Since Derrida wishes to contribute to the demise of that epoch, his work cannot admit a notion of history that has perhaps served as a prop or a refuge for logocentric thought. While Jauss seeks to refurbish history in order to challenge the study of literature, Derrida wants to banish history in order to read more correctly the logocentric text. Jauss seeks a reversal in the relationship of cultural histories to general history; Derrida sees both varieties as symptoms and relics of a larger philosophical issue.

Poetics and historiography: Hayden White

But even less radical members of the critical "avant-garde" take a position that has seemed more revolutionary than Jauss's when it comes to challenging traditional historiography. Perhaps the best-known writer in the English-speaking world to deal with these questions has been Hayden White.[1] Like Jauss, White also disputes the existence of objective historical facts and ends up, it can be argued, with a similarly relativized view of history that excludes notions of truth and certainty. The way in which he develops his metahistorical outlook, however, again shows the gap between reception theory and other contemporary trends.

For White depends most heavily on the conception of historical writing as narrative and on poetic theory for his critique. In analyzing various narrative strategies employed by historians, he observes a series of fourfold typologies according to the mode of emplotment, the mode of explanation, and the mode of ideological implication. Although none of these modes has its origin in purely personal factors (and is thus not relative in the sense of arbitrary), it is impossible to assign priority to any particular plot, explanation, or ideology. White's point is that reading and writing history are in essential ways analogous to writing a story. Like the medieval poet, the historian is restricted by the tropes and conventions of his/her trade more than by the "truth" of the presentation.

What White's model establishes, therefore, is the proximity of history to literature, and the most controversial and stimulating aspects of his theory come when he makes this connection explicit. By labeling the modes of emplotment with terms drawn from poetics – romance, comedy, tragedy, and satire – and by ascribing rhetorical tropes to explanatory models – metaphor, metonymy, synecdoche, and irony – White suggests a fictional dimension and ultimately a linguistic determinacy to our understanding of the past. In contrast to Jauss's discussion of historiography, White is thus more differentiated, more radical, and more literary. While Jauss bases his revised conception of history on a dialogic relationship with the past, White encompasses all historiography under categories of narrative. Whereas the aesthetics of reception seeks to incorporate past interpretation into the unfolding and writing of history, the metahistorical view conceives of all histories as fundamentally interpretive acts. And while Jauss proposes that the cultural approach to history can henceforth serve as a paradigm for general histories, White counters with a model in which literary tropes enable historical thought itself. Jauss's project, in short, strives to place history at the center of literary studies; White's, by contrast, calls history itself into question by placing literary studies at the center of historiography.

Renewing the provocation

To a degree it is unfair to compare White's theory with Jauss's in this area. White, after all, is a writer who has specialized in historiography, while Jauss is a Romance-language scholar interested in revitalizing his academic discipline with new notions of literary history. The point here and throughout this chapter, however, concerns the way in which certain problems have been conceptualized by reception theorists and other contemporary critics. The comparisons between recent German views and the so-called avant-garde in France and the United States were not meant to demonstrate the superiority of one set of approaches. Rather, in the first instance, they were designed to highlight some of the theoretical limitations that reception theory has encountered over the past few years, to show where reception theorists have faced significant problems in establishing a "new paradigm."

But the preceding remarks on the text, the reader, interpretation, and literary history may serve secondarily as a partial account of the difficulties reception theory has had – and will continue to have – in gaining acceptance in contemporary critical circles outside Germany. Indeed, as the positions outlined above document, reception theory can appear as a conservative enterprise: from the perspective of the "avant-garde" this critical school retains or reintroduces a good portion of the baggage carried by the tradition that it purports to overturn.

Thus far reception theorists have been slow to take up the challenges implicit in French and American critical discourse. Although Jauss specializes in French literature and Iser has close connections with the academic world in the United States, one rarely finds in their writings references to the dominant literary theories in these countries. The two major works by Iser and Jauss, *The Act of Reading* and *Aesthetic Experience and Literary Hermeneutics*, contain no mention of Derrida or Lacan; and Foucault is included only in a passing footnote by Iser. American disciples of French thought fare no better in these volumes. Reception theorists, in short, have generally avoided the very issues that have proved to be most provocative outside Germany.

This may change now that post-structuralism is gaining some minimal foothold among younger German scholars – although for institutional reasons this branch of theory will probably remain marginal in Germany for some time. Even if they are not confronted by an internal challenge, however, it would still be desirable for reception theorists to enter into a dialogue with other popular currents of criticism.

Given the present mutual lack of familiarity, such a dialogue might be of benefit to all parties, forcing them to rethink what have become the respective clichés of their critical discourse. The reception of reception theory in the English-speaking world, until now a restricted matter, may thus lie in the future. For if it can enter into a productive relationship with other modes of contemporary thought, reception theory could again provide, as it has provided for a generation of German critics, a welcome "provocation" to literary scholarship.

Notes

Preface

1 Hans Robert Jauss, "Esthétique de la réception et communication littéraire," in *Literary Communication and Reception: Proceedings of the IXth Congress of the International Comparative Literature Association*, Innsbrucker Beiträge zur Kulturwissenschaft, Sonderheft 46 (Innsbruck: Verlag des Instituts für Sprachwissenschaft der Universität Innsbruck, 1980), p. 15.

2 Susan Suleiman and Inge Crosman (eds), *The Reader in the Text: Essays on Audience and Interpretation* (Princeton: Princeton University Press, 1980); and Jane P. Tompkins (ed.), *Reader-Response Criticism: From Formalism to Post-Structuralism* (Baltimore and London: Johns Hopkins University Press, 1980).

3 *Poetik und Hermeneutik: Arbeitsergebnisse einer Forschungsgruppe* (Munich: Fink, 1964ff.).

Chapter 1 The change in paradigm and its socio-historical function

Paradigms in the history of criticism

1 Hans Robert Jauss, "Paradigmawechsel in der Literaturwissenschaft," *Linguistische Berichte*, no. 3, 1969, pp. 44–56.

Scientific revolutions and literary scholarship

1 Thomas S. Kuhn, *The Structure of Scientific Revolutions*, second enlarged edn, International Encyclopedia of Unified Science,

vol. 2, no. 2 (Chicago: University of Chicago Press, 1970), p. 208.

2   *Rezeptionsgeschichte: Grundlegung einer Theorie* (Munich: Fink, 1977).

3   Zoran Konstantinović, Manfred Naumann, and Hans Robert Jauss (eds), *Literary Communication and Reception: Proceedings of the IXth Congress of the International Comparative Literature Association*, Innsbrucker Beiträge zur Kulturwissenschaft, Sonderheft 46 (Innsbruck: Verlag des Instituts für Sprachwissenschaft der Universität Innsbruck, 1980).

4   Jürgen Kolbe (ed.), *Ansichten einer künftigen Germanistik* (Munich: Hanser, 1969).

5   Jürgen Kolbe (ed.), *Neue Ansichten einer künftigen Germanistik* (Munich: Hanser, 1973).

6   Wolfgang Kayser, *Das sprachliche Kunstwerk: Eine Einführung in die Literaturwissenschaft*, fourteenth edn (Bern: Francke, 1969); and Emil Staiger, *Die Kunst der Interpretation: Studien zur deutschen Literaturgeschichte*, fifth edn (Zurich: Artemis, 1967).

Chapter 2   Influences and precursors

Russian Formalism

1   Unless otherwise indicated, quotations cited parenthetically in the text refer to the two-volume *Texte der russischen Formalisten*, eds Jurij Striedter and Wolf-Dieter Stempel (Munich: Fink, 1969 and 1972).

2   Boris Tomashevskii, "Literature and biography," in Ladislav Matejka and Krystyna Pomorska (eds), *Readings in Russian Poetics* (Cambridge, Mass.: MIT Press, 1971), pp. 47–55. All quotations in this paragraph refer to this essay.

3   Fredric Jameson, *The Prison-House of Language: A Critical Account of Structuralism and Russian Formalism* (Princeton: Princeton University Press, 1972), p. 53.

4   Quoted from Boris M. Eikhenbaum, "The theory of the formal method," in *Readings in Russian Poetics*, p. 32.

5   This is the phrase Jauss uses in his "Provocation" essay; see Hans Robert Jauss, *Toward an Aesthetic of Reception*, trans. Timothy Bahti (Minneapolis: University of Minnesota Press, 1982), p. 33.

Roman Ingarden

1   Roman Ingarden, *The Literary Work of Art: An Investigation on the Borderlines of Ontology, Logic, and Theory of Literature*, trans. George

G. Grabowicz (Evanston, Ill.: Northwestern University Press, 1973), pp. lxii–lxiii.
2   See René Wellek and Austin Warren, *Theory of Literature*, third edn (New York: Harcourt, Brace & World, 1956).
3   This volume, originally published in Polish in 1937 and in German in 1968, was translated into English by Ruth Ann Crowly and Kenneth R. Olsen (Evanston, Ill.: Northwestern University Press, 1973).
4   Here and in other passages in this section I have profited from reading Eugene H. Falk, *The Poetics of Roman Ingarden* (Chapel Hill: University of North Carolina Press, 1981).

Prague structuralism (Jan Mukařovský and Felix Vodička)

1   I am referring to *The Word and Verbal Act: Selected Essays by Jan Mukařovský* and the companion volume *Structure, Sign, and Function*; both were edited and translated by John Burbank and Peter Steiner (New Haven and London: Yale University Press, 1977 and 1978).
2   Trans. Mark E. Suino (Ann Arbor, Mich.: University of Michigan, 1970).
3   See "Die Literaturgeschichte, ihre Probleme und Aufgaben," in Felix Vodička, *Die Struktur der literarischen Entwicklung*, trans. Tuschinsky *et al.* (Munich: Fink, 1976), pp. 30–86, especially pp. 60–73. The section on literary reception in this essay appeared in English under the title "The history of the echo of literary works," in Paul L. Garvin (trans. and ed.), *A Prague School Reader on Esthetics, Literary Structure, and Style* (Washington, DC: Georgetown University Press, 1964), pp. 71–81.
4   See "The concretization of the literary work," in Peter Steiner (ed.), *The Prague School: Selected Writings 1929–1946* (Austin: University of Texas Press, 1982), pp. 103–34.

Hans-Georg Gadamer

1   The most recent German version of *Wahrheit und Methode* (Tübingen: Mohr, 1972) is an expanded version of the original 1960 edition. The English translation by Garrett Barden and John Cumming (New York: Continuum, 1975), which will be cited parenthetically in this section, used the second edition (1965) and thus does not contain Gadamer's epilogue (*Nachwort*).
2   Gadamer, *Philosophical Hermeneutics*, trans. and ed. David E. Linge (Berkeley: University of California Press, 1976), p. 37.

3 Gadamer, *Wahrheit und Methode* (*Nachwort*), p. 514.

4 Martin Heidegger, *Being and Time*, trans. John Macquarrie and Edward Robinson (New York: Harper & Row, 1962).

Sociology of literature

1 Leo Löwenthal, *Erzählkunst und Gesellschaft: Die Gesellschaftsproblematik in der deutschen Literatur des 19. Jahrhunderts* (Neuwied: Luchterhand, 1971), p. 39.

2 Leo Löwenthal, "Die Auffassung Dostojewskis im Vorkriegsdeutschland," *Zeitschrift für Sozialforschung*, no. 3, 1934, pp. 343–82. Hereafter cited parenthetically in the text. An abbreviated English translation with the title "The reception of Dostoevski's work in Germany: 1880–1920" appeared in Robert Neal Wilson (ed.), *The Arts in Society* (Englewood Cliffs, NJ: Prentice Hall, 1964), pp. 122–47.

3 Julian Hirsch, *Die Genesis des Ruhmes: Ein Beitrag zur Methodenlehre der Geschichte* (Leipzig: Johann Ambrosius Barth, 1914). Hereafter cited parenthetically in the text.

4 Levin L. Schücking, *The Sociology of Literary Taste*, trans. Brian Battershaw (London: Routledge & Kegan Paul, 1966), p. 90. Hereafter cited parenthetically in the text.

5 Levin L. Schücking, "Literaturgeschichte und Geschmacksgeschichte," *Germanisch-romanische Monatsschrift*, no. 5, 1913, pp. 561–77; here p. 564.

Chapter 3 The major theorists

From the history of reception to aesthetic experience: Hans Robert Jauss

1 Hans Robert Jauss, *Literaturgeschichte als Provokation* (Frankfurt: Suhrkamp, 1970), p. 7.

2 This essay has been rendered into English with the title "Literary history as a challenge to literary theory" in the volume Hans Robert Jauss, *Toward an Aesthetic of Reception*, trans. Timothy Bahti (Minneapolis: University of Minnesota Press, 1982), pp. 3–45. With minor alterations for the sake of accuracy, I shall be quoting from this volume. Further references to it will appear parenthetically in the text.

3 Jauss, *Literaturgeschichte*, p. 9.

4 Hans-Georg Gadamer, *Truth and Method* (New York: Continuum, 1975), p. 269.

5 E. H. Gombrich, *Art and Illusion* (Princeton: Princeton University Press, 1960), p. 66.

6   See Hans Robert Jauss, *Untersuchungen zur mittelalterlichen Tierdicht-ung* (Tübingen: Niemeyer, 1959), pp. 153, 180, 225, and 271; and review of *La Littérature et le lecteur*, by Arthur Nisin, *Archiv für das Studium der neuen Sprachen*, vol. 197, 1961, pp. 223–5.

7   Hans Robert Jauss, "Der Leser als Instanz einer neuen Geschich-te der Literatur," *Poetica*, vol. 7, no. 3–4, 1975, pp. 325–44; here, p. 327.

8   The original German version of this book was *Ästhetische Erfahrung und literarische Hermeneutik* (Munich: Fink, 1977).

9   Constance: Universitätsverlag, 1972.

10   Citations are from Theodor Adorno, *Ästhetische Theorie* (Frankfurt: Suhrkamp, 1970).

11   Unless otherwise noted, further parenthetical citations will refer to *Aesthetic Experience and Literary Hermeneutics*, trans. Michael Shaw (Minneapolis: University of Minnesota Press, 1982). Some quotes have been slightly altered. See footnote 8 for original German title.

12   Roland Barthes, *The Pleasure of the Text* (*Le Plaisir du texte*, Paris: Seuil, 1973), trans. Richard Miller, with a note on the text by Richard Howard (London: Cape, 1975).

13   Princeton and London: Princeton University Press, 1957.

14   The same could be said for Jauss's most recent theoretical state-ment in the revised and expanded edition of *Ästhetische Erfahrung und literarische Hermeneutik* (Frankfurt: Suhrkamp, 1982). Here Jauss reconsiders some of his earlier concerns, notably the "hor-izon of expectations" (pp. 657–703). Although the horizon is now more firmly connected with phenomenological theory, Jauss still has not completely overcome the objectivist dilemma noted above.

Textuality and the reader's response: Wolfgang Iser

1   The English version appeared in J. Hillis Miller (ed.), *Aspects of Narrative: Selected Papers from the English Institute* (New York and London: Columbia University Press, 1971), pp. 1–45.

2   Further references to *The Act of Reading: A Theory of Aesthetic Response* (Baltimore and London: Johns Hopkins University Press, 1978) will be noted parenthetically.

3   Wolfgang Iser, *The Implied Reader: Patterns of Communication in Prose Fiction from Bunyan to Beckett* (Baltimore and London: Johns Hop-kins University Press, 1974).

4   See Wayne C. Booth, *The Rhetoric of Fiction* (Chicago and London: University of Chicago Press, 1961).

5   Wolfgang Iser, "Im Lichte der Kritik," in Rainer Warning (ed.), *Rezeptionsästhetik: Theorie und Praxis* (Munich: Fink, 1975), pp. 325–42; here, p. 335.

6 Wolfgang Iser, "The pattern of negativity in Beckett's prose," *Georgia Review*, vol. 29, no. 3, 1975, pp. 706–19; here, p. 719.

7 Wallace Martin, review of *The Act of Reading*, by Wolfgang Iser, *Criticism*, vol. 21, 1979, p. 262.

8 Stanley Fish, "Why no one's afraid of Wolfgang Iser," *Diacritics*, vol. 11, no. 1, 1981, pp. 2–13.

9 Wolfgang Iser, "Talk like whales," *Diacritics*, vol. 11, no. 3, 1981, pp. 82–7.

Chapter 4 Alternative models and controversies

The communication model: levels of text-reader interaction

1 Jürgen Habermas, *Theorie des kommunikativen Handelns*, 2 vols (Frankfurt: Suhrkamp, 1981).

2 Rien T. Segers, "An interview with Hans Robert Jauss," *New Literary History*, vol. 11, no. 1, 1979, pp. 83–95.

3 Wolfgang Iser, "The current situation of literary theory: key concepts and the imaginary," *New Literary History*, vol. 11, no. 1, 1979, pp. 1–20.

4 Hans Ulrich Gumbrecht, "Konsequenzen der Rezeptionsästhetik oder Literaturwissenschaft als Kommunikationssoziologie," *Poetica*, vol. 7, no. 3–4, 1975, pp. 388–413.

5 Karlheinz Stierle, "The reading of fictional texts," in Susan R. Suleiman and Inge Crosman (eds), *The Reader in the Text: Essays on Audience and Interpretation* (Princeton: Princeton University Press, 1980), pp. 83–105; here, p. 88.

6 Karlheinz Stierle, *Text als Handlung: Perspektiven einer systematischen Literaturwissenschaft* (Munich: Fink, 1975). Hereafter cited parenthetically in the text.

7 Rolf Grimminger, "Abriss einer Theorie der literarischen Kommunikation," *Linguistik und Didaktik*, vol. 3, no. 4, 1972, pp. 277–93; and vol. 4, no. 1, 1973, pp. 1–15.

8 Günter Waldmann, *Kommunikationsästhetik I: Die Ideologie der Erzählform* (Munich: Fink, 1976).

Marxist reception theory: the east–west debate

1 Manfred Naumann, "Literatur und Leser," *Weimarer Beiträge*, vol. 16, no. 5, 1970, pp. 92–116; Claus Träger, "Zur Kritik der bürgerlichen Literaturwissenschaft," *Weimarer Beiträge*, vol. 18, no. 2, 1972, pp. 10–42, and no. 3, 1972, pp. 10–36; and Robert Weimann, "'Rezeptionsästhetik' und die Krise der Literaturgeschichte: Zur Kritik einer neuen Strömung in der bürgerlichen

Literaturwissenschaft," *Weimarer Beiträge*, vol. 19, no. 8, 1973, pp. 5–33. Weimann's essay appeared in English with the title "'Reception asethetics' and the crisis in literary history," trans. Charles Spencer, *Clio*, vol. 5, no. 1, 1975, pp. 3–31.

2   This volume was authored by a collective consisting of Dieter Schlenstedt, Karlheinz Barck, Dieter Kliche, and Rosemarie Lenzer under the direction of Manfred Naumann. It was published in Weimar and Berlin by Aufbau-Verlag. A translation of pp. 17–29 and 83–97 has appeared as "Literary production and reception" in *New Literary History*, vol. 8, no. 1, 1976, pp. 107–26.

3   Quoted from the *Marx–Engels Reader*, ed. Robert C. Tucker (New York: Norton, 1972), pp. 4–5.

4   Quoted from Karl Marx and Fredrick Engels, *The German Ideology* (New York: International Publishers, 1970), p. 150.

5   See Michael Nerlich, "Romanistik und Anti-Kommunismus," *Das Argument*, vol. 14, no. 3–4, 1972, pp. 276–313.

6   *Gesellschaft–Literatur–Lesen*, pp. 18–34. A partial English translation appears in Naumann, "Literary production and reception," pp. 107–14.

7   See Hans Robert Jauss, *Toward an Aesthetic of Reception*, trans. Timothy Bahti (Minneapolis: University of Minnesota Press, 1982), p. 21.

8   Hans Robert Jauss, "Racines und Goethes Iphigenie: Mit einem Nachwort über die Partialität der rezeptionsästhetischen Methode," in Rainer Warning (ed.), *Rezeptionsästhetik: Theorie und Praxis* (Munich: Fink, 1975), pp. 353–400; here, pp. 381–2.

9   Wolfgang Iser, "Im Lichte der Kritik," in *Rezeptionsästhetik*, pp. 325–42; here, p. 341.

10 Hans Robert Jauss, "The idealist embarrassment: observations on Marxist aesthetics," *New Literary History*, vol. 7, no. 1, 1975, pp. 191–208; here, p. 202.

Empirical reception theory: actual responses to texts

1   See Dieter Schlenstedt *et al.* (eds), *Literarische Widerspiegelung: Geschichtliche und theoretische Dimensionen eines Problems* (Berlin and Weimar: Aufbau-Verlag, 1981).

2   Dietrich Sommer and Dietrich Löffler, "Soziologische Probleme der literarischen Wirkungsforschung," *Weimarer Beiträge*, vol. 16, no. 8, 1970, pp. 51–76.

3   Dietrich Sommer *et al.* (eds), *Funktion und Wirkung: Soziologische Untersuchungen zur Literatur und Kunst* (Berlin and Weimar: Aufbau-Verlag, 1978).

4   Reinhold Viehoff, "Über einen Versuch, den Erwartungshorizont

zeitgenössischer Literaturkritik empirisch zu objektivieren," *Zeitschrift für Literaturwissenschaft und Linguistik*, vol. 6, no. 21, 1976, pp. 96–124.

5 In *Literaturpsychologie: Literaturwissenschaft zwischen Hermeneutik und Empirie* (Stuttgart: Kohlhammer, 1972) p. 18.

6 Norbert Groeben, "Die Kommunikativität moderner deutscher Lyrik," *Sprache im technischen Zeitalter*, no. 34, 1970, pp. 83–105.

7 Heinz Hillmann, "Rezeption–empirisch," in Walter Müller-Seidel (ed.), *Historizität in Sprach- und Literaturwissenschaft* (Munich: Fink, 1974), pp. 433–49.

8 Werner Faulstich, *Domänen der Rezeptionsanalyse: Probleme–Lösungsstrategien–Ergebnisse* (Kronberg/Ts.: Athenäum, 1977), pp. 32–117.

9 Werner Bauer *et al.*, *Text und Rezeption: Wirkungsanalyse zeitgenössischer Lyrik am Beispiel des Gedichts "Fadensonnen" von Paul Celan* (Frankfurt: Athenäum, 1972).

10 The German original appeared in Celan's *Atemwende* (Frankfurt: Suhrkamp, 1967), p. 22; the translation is from Paul Celan, *Poems*, trans. Michael Hamburger (New York: Persea, 1980), p. 183.

Chapter 5 Problems and perspectives

1 Hans Robert Jauss, *Ästhetische Erfahrung und literarische Hermeneutik* (Frankfurt: Suhrkamp, 1982).

The disappearing text: Stanley Fish

1 Fish's essays on literary theory from the 1970s are collected in *Is There a Text in This Class? The Authority of Interpretive Communities* (Cambridge, Mass.: Harvard University Press, 1980).

The rise of the reader

1 Erwin Wolff, "Der intendierte Leser: Überlegungen und Beispiele zur Einführung eines literaturwissenschaftlichen Begriffs," *Poetica*, vol. 4, no. 2, 1971, pp. 141–66.

2 The title of an essay by Jauss that appeared in *Poetica*, vol. 7, no. 3–4, 1975, pp. 325–44, was "Der Leser als Instanz einer neuen Geschichte der Literatur."

The decentered reader: Roland Barthes

1 Roland Barthes, *S/Z*, trans. Richard Miller (New York: Hill and Wang, 1974). All quotes are from p. 10.

Interpretation and the search for meaning

1 Wolfgang Iser, *The Act of Reading: A Theory of Aesthetic Response* (Baltimore and London: Johns Hopkins University Press, 1978).
2 Jonathan Culler, *Structuralist Poetics: Structuralism, Linguistics, and the Study of Literature* (Ithaca, NY: Cornell University Press, 1975), p. 118.

The necessity of misinterpretation: Harold Bloom

1 Harold Bloom, *The Anxiety of Influence: A Theory of Poetry* (Oxford: Oxford University Press, 1973), pp. 94–5.

Reconstituting literary history

1 Hans Robert Jauss, *Toward an Aesthetic of Reception*, trans. Timothy Bahti (Minneapolis: University of Minnesota Press, 1982), p. 62. This quote appears in the important essay "History of art and pragmatic history," originally published in 1970.

History as metaphysics: Jacques Derrida

1 Jacques Derrida, *Of Grammatology*, trans. Gayatri Chakravorty Spivak (Baltimore and London: Johns Hopkins University Press, 1976).

Poetics and historiography: Hayden White

1 See especially his *Metahistory: The Historical Imagination in Nineteenth Century Europe* (Baltimore and London: Johns Hopkins University Press, 1973).

Select bibliography

I have divided this bibliography into four sections. The first three correspond roughly to material discussed in chapters 2(A), 3 and 4(B), and 5(C). The final section lists relevant periodicals and special issues on reception theory.

Only a fraction of the material that I consulted is listed below. Primary sources predominate; only a few items from the vast amount of secondary literature were included. Throughout I have given preference to volumes that have appeared in English. For a more comprehensive bibliography of works that appeared through 1977, see Gunter Grimm's bibliography in *Rezeptionsgeschichte*, cited below in B.

A Precursors and influences

1   ERLICH, VICTOR, *Russian Formalism: History Doctrine*, second revised edn, Slavistic Printings and Reprintings, 4 (The Hague: Mouton, 1965). Most comprehensive and informed study of Russian Formalism.

2   FALK, EUGENE H., *The Poetics of Roman Ingarden* (Chapel Hill: University of North Carolina Press, 1981). Useful commentary on Ingarden, although it lacks critical distance.

3   GADAMER, HANS-GEORG, *Truth and Method*, trans. Garrett Barden and John Cumming (New York: Continuum, 1975). Gadamer's *magnum opus*; seeks to renew the hermeneutical tradition in opposition to the "method" in the natural sciences and its claim to "truth." Translation of second edn.

4 ——, *Philosophical Hermeneutics*, trans. and ed. David E. Linge (Berkeley: University of California Press, 1976). Selected essays that clarify positions in his major work. Excellent introduction by Linge.

5 GARVIN, PAUL L. (ed. and trans.), *A Prague School Reader on Esthetics, Literary Structure, and Style* (Washington, DC: Georgetown University Press, 1964). Contains a variety of essays from the Prague School including Mukařovský's "Standard language and poetic language" and Vodička's "The history of the echo of literary works."

6 HIRSCH, JULIAN, *Die Genesis des Ruhmes: Ein Beitrag zur Methodenlehre der Geschichte* (Leipzig: Johann Ambrosius Barth, 1914). Unusual volume on historiography that examines "fame" from the perspective of reception.

7 HOY, DAVID COUZENS, *The Critical Circle: Literature, History, and Philosophical Hermeneutics* (Berkeley: University of California Press, 1978). Excellent introduction to the central issues in hermeneutical theory. Tends to be more modern and critical than Palmer.

8 INGARDEN, ROMAN, *The Cognition of the Literary Work of Art*, trans. Ruth Ann Crowly and Kenneth R. Olsen (Evanston, Ill.: Northwestern University Press, 1973). Originally published in Polish in 1937, then in German in 1968, this volume focuses on the reception of literary works. Most influential for Iser among reception theorists.

9 ——, *The Literary Work of Art: An Investigation on the Borderlines of Ontology, Logic, and Theory of Literature*, trans. George G. Grabowicz (Evanston, Ill.: Northwestern University Press, 1973). Originally appeared in German in 1931. Analyzes the strata of the literary work of art from a phenomenological perspective. Concentration on work itself responsible for Ingarden's "formalist" reputation.

10 JAMESON, FREDRIC, *The Prison-House of Language: A Critical Account of Structuralism and Russian Formalism* (Princeton: Princeton University Press, 1972). An excellent introduction to two important movements.

11 LEMON, LEE T., and REIS, MARION J. (trans.), *Russian Formalist Criticism: Four Essays* (Lincoln, Nebraska: University of Nebraska Press, 1965). Contains several important essays, including Shklovskii's "Art as technique." Unfortunately translations are not always accurate.

12 LÖWENTHAL, LEO, "Die Auffassung Dostojewskis im Vorkriegsdeutschland," *Zeitschrift für Sozialforschung*, no. 3, 1934, pp. 343–82. Exemplary study of reception from a psycho-sociological

perspective. An abbreviated English translation with the title "The reception of Dostoevski's work in Germany: 1880–1920" appeared in Robert Neal Wilson (ed.), *The Arts in Society* (Englewood Cliffs, NJ: Prentice Hall, 1964), pp. 122–47.

13 MATEJKA, LADISLAV, and POMORSKA, KRYSTYNA (eds), *Readings in Russian Poetics: Formalist and Structuralist Views* (Cambridge, Mass.: MIT Press, 1971). A useful volume of Formalist writings on literary topics. Broader and more accurate than Lemon and Reis.

14 MUKAŘOVSKÝ, JAN, *Aesthetic Function, Norm and Value as Social Facts*, trans. Mark E. Suino (Ann Arbor: University of Michigan Press, 1970). Perhaps Mukařovský's most important theoretical piece. Originally published in 1934

15 ——, *The Word and Verbal Act: Selected Essays by Jan Mukařovský*, trans. John Burbank and Peter Steiner (New Haven and London: Yale University Press, 1977). Together with *Structure, Sign, and Function*, a good selection of Mukařovský's work in English. Mukařovský, the leading literary theorist in the Prague Structuralist Circle, has been unfortunately neglected in the English-speaking world.

16 ——, *Structure, Sign, and Function*, trans. John Burbank and Peter Steiner (New Haven and London: Yale University Press, 1978). Collection of essays focusing on semiotic and structuralist aspects of Mukařovský's work. Extremely useful bibliography of both Czech works and translations (pp. 251–66).

17 PALMER, RICHARD E., *Hermeneutics: Interpretation Theory in Schleiermacher, Dilthey, Heidegger, and Gadamer* (Evanston, Ill.: Northwestern University Press, 1969). Extremely useful introduction to the hermeneutical tradition in the past two centuries. Tends to take a Gadamerian perspective.

18 SARTRE, JEAN-PAUL, *What Is Literature?*, trans. Bernard Frechtman (New York: Harper & Row, 1965). In discussing the committed writer, Sartre often refers to matters that became of central concern in reception theory (e.g. the "structure of appeal" in literary texts).

19 SCHÜCKING, LEVIN L., *The Sociology of Literary Taste*, trans. Brian Battershaw (London: Routledge & Kegan Paul, 1966). Originally published in German in 1931, this is one of the first and most important studies in the sociology of reception.

20 STEINER, PETER (ed.), *The Prague School: Selected Writings 1929–1946* (Austin: University of Texas Press, 1982). Wide range of essays from the Prague Linguistic Circle. Includes Vodička's important reception-related comments in "The concretization of the literary work" as well as Mukařovský's "Structuralism in

esthetics and in literary studies." Closing essay by Steiner discussed the history of the Circle.

21 STEMPEL, WOLF-DIETER (ed.), *Texte der russischen Formalisten*, vol. II (Munich: Fink, 1972).

22 STRIEDTER, JURIJ (ed.), *Texte der russischen Formalisten*, vol. I (Munich: Fink, 1969). Russian text with facing German translations. With volume II best collection of essays by the Formalists in a western language.

23 VODIČKA, FELIX, *Die Struktur der literarischen Entwicklung*, trans. Christian Tuschinsky, Peter Richter, and Frank Boldt, Theorie und Geschichte der Literatur und der schönen Künste, 34 (Munich: Fink, 1976). An important collection of essays by Mukařovský's student. To a degree a systematic presentation of his mentor's views.

B Reception theory

24 AMACHER, RICHARD, and LANGE, VICTOR (eds), *New Perspectives in German Literary Criticism* (Princeton: Princeton University Press, 1979). Selected essays from the first five volumes of the series *Poetik und Hermeneutik* (see below).

25 BAUER, WERNER, *et al.*, *Text und Rezeption: Wirkungsanalyse zeitgenössischer Lyrik am Beispiel des Gedichts "Fadensonnen" von Paul Celan* (Frankfurt: Athenäum, 1972). Extensive empirical analysis of one poem. See pp. 143–5.

26 BÜRGER, PETER, *Theorie der Avantgarde* (Frankfurt: Suhrkamp, 1974). Introduces the useful notion of the "institution" to deal with changes in production and reception. Influential work in Germany during the 1970s. To appear in English translation (University of Minnesota Press).

27 ENGELSING, ROLF, *Analphabetentum und Lektüre: Zur Sozialgeschichte des Lesers in Deutschland zwischen feudaler und industrieller Gesellschaft* (Stuttgart: Metzler, 1973). Studies of reading habits, literacy, and popular literature in the eighteenth and nineteenth centuries.

28 FAULSTICH, WERNER, *Domänen der Rezeptionsanalyse* (Kronberg/Ts.: Athenäum, 1977). Five empirical studies of reception. See pp. 142–3.

29 GRIMM, GUNTER (ed.), *Literatur und Leser: Theorien und Modelle zur Rezeption literarischer Werke* (Stuttgart: Reclam, 1975). Long, helpful introductory essay by Grimm is followed by three theoretical essays and ten applications. Good bibliography.

30 ——, *Rezeptionsgeschichte: Grundlegung einer Theorie* (Munich: Fink, 1977). Long initial essay reviews and critiques the major positions

in reception theory. Four sample analyses follow. Extensive (66 pages) bibliography makes this book invaluable.

31 GRIMMINGER, ROLF, "Abriss einer Theorie der literarischen Kommunikation," *Linguistik und Didaktik*, vol. 3, no. 4, 1972, pp. 277–93; and vol. 4, no. 1, 1973, pp. 1–15. See pp. 115–16.

32 GROEBEN, NORBERT, *Rezeptionsforschung als empirische Literaturwissenschaft: Paradigma- durch Methodendiskussion an Untersuchungsbeispielen* (Kronberg/Ts.: Athenäum, 1977). Comprehensive statement of the empirical position from one of its foremost advocates.

33 GUMBRECHT, HANS ULRICH, "Konsequenzen der Rezeptionsästhetik oder Literaturwissenschaft als Kommunikationssoziologie," *Poetica*, vol. 7, no. 3 4, 1975, pp. 388 413. Attempt to place reception theory in the framework of a sociology of communication.

34 HEUERMANN, HARTMUT, *et al.* (eds), *Literarische Rezeption: Beiträge zur Theorie des Text–Leser-Verhältnisses und seiner Erforschung* (Paderborn: Schöningh, 1975). Fourteen essays from an empirical perspective.

35 HOHENDAHL, PETER UWE (ed.), *Sozialgeschichte und Wirkungsästhetik: Dokumente zur empirischen und marxistischen Rezeptionsforschung* (Frankfurt: Athenäum, 1974). Excellent reader on non-Constance School contributions to reception theory.

36 ——, "Introduction to reception aesthetics," *New German Critique*, no. 10, 1977, pp. 29–63. English translation of introduction to *Sozialgeschichte und Wirkungsästhetik*. Good overview of history of empirical, sociological, and Marxist research in reception.

37 ——, *The Institution of Criticism* (Ithaca, NY: Cornell University Press, 1982). Collection of essays on the institutional aspects of literature and the relationship between literary criticism and the public sphere.

38 ISER, WOLFGANG, "Indeterminacy and the reader's response," in J. Hillis Miller (ed.), *Aspects of Narrative: Selected Papers from the English Institute* (New York and London: Columbia University Press, 1971), pp. 1–45. Originally delivered as a lecture at Constance in 1970, this essay is an early outline of Iser's theory of reader response.

39 ——, *The Implied Reader: Patterns of Communication in Prose Fiction from Bunyan to Beckett* (Baltimore and London: Johns Hopkins University Press, 1974). German original in 1972. Individual analyses of prose works from various centuries. English volume includes theoretical piece "The reading process: a phenomenological approach" as the last chapter.

40 ——, *The Act of Reading: A Theory of Aesthetic Response* (Baltimore

and London: Johns Hopkins University Press, 1978). German original in 1976. Iser's most extensive theoretical work. For a summary and discussion of this book, see pp. 83–96.

41 ———, "The current situation of literary theory: key concepts and the imaginary," *New Literary History*, vol. 11, no. 1, 1979, pp. 1–20. Iser surveys current criticism using the concepts of structure, function, and communication; see pp. 109–10.

42 JAUSS, HANS ROBERT, "Paradigmawechsel in der Literaturwissenschaft," *Linguistische Berichte*, no. 3, 1969, pp. 44–56. Attempt to harness Kuhn's theory of scientific revolutions ror literary scholarship; see pp. 1–4

43 ———, *Kleine Apologie der ästhetischen Erfahrung*, Konstanzer Universitätsreden, 59 (Constance: Universitätsverlag, 1972). Marks Jauss's turn from an aesthetics of negativity to a concern with the spectrum of aesthetic experience. Superseded by the initial essay in *Aesthetic Experience and Literary Hermeneutics*.

44 ———, "The idealist embarrassment: observations on Marxist aesthetics," *New Literary History*, vol. 7, no. 1, 1975, pp. 191–208. Jauss on Marxist aesthetics and his GDR detractors.

45 ———, "Der Leser als Instanz einer neuen Geschichte der Literatur," *Poetica*, vol. 7, no. 3–4, 1975, pp. 325–44. Jauss sums up achievements of reception theory to this point, corrects his earlier theory, and answers his critics.

46 ———, *Aesthetic Experience and Literary Hermeneutics*, trans. Michael Shaw (Minneapolis: University of Minnesota Press, 1982). Originally published in German in 1977. Represents Jauss's revision of his initial aesthetics of reception. Pleasure, identification, and affirmation are integrated into his model here. The first two essays, "A sketch of a theory and history of aesthetic experience" and "Interaction patterns of identification with the hero," outline the new theory. A revised and expanded edition appeared in German (Frankfurt: Suhrkamp) in 1982. For my discussion of the initial publication under this title, see pp. 70–81.

47 ———, *Toward an Aesthetic of Reception*, trans. Timothy Bahti (Minneapolis: University of Minnesota Press, 1982). Collection of important essays by Jauss including his manifesto of the aesthetics of reception, "Literary history as a challenge to literary theory." Originally delivered as a speech at Constance in 1967, this essay is one of the central documents of reception theory. Other essays include "History of art and pragmatic history," "Theory of genres and medieval history," "Goethe's and Valéry's *Faust*," and "The poetic text within the change of horizons of reading."

48 KRUEZER, HELMUT, "Trivialliteratur als Forschungsproblem: Zur Kritik des deutschen Trivialromans seit der Aufklä-

rung," *Deutsche Vierteljahrsschrift*, vol. 41, 1967, pp. 173–91. Pioneering essay suggesting a re-examination of our notion of *Trivialliteratur* (popular or pulp literature) from the perspective of social reception.

49 LINK, HANNELORE, "'Die Appellstruktur der Texte' und 'ein Paradigmawechsel in der Literaturwissenschaft,'" *Jahrbuch der deutschen Schillergesellschaft*, vol. 17, 1973, pp. 532–83. Criticism of Iser's early theory, especially for its failure to break with traditional practices.

50 ——, *Rezeptionsforschung: Eine Einführung in Methoden und Probleme* (Stuttgart: Kohlhammer, 1976). One of the best introductions to general problems in reception theory.

51 MANDELKOW, KARL ROBERT, "Probleme der Wirkungsästhetik," *Jahrbuch für Internationale Germanistik*, vol. 2, 1970, pp. 71–84. Suggestions for refining conceptual apparatus of reception theory; calls for a greater differentiation in the "horizon of expectations."

52 NAUMANN, MANFRED, "Das Dilemma der 'Rezeptionsästhetik,'" *Poetica*, vol. 8, no. 3–4, 1976, pp. 451–66. Interesting overview of the problems in reception theory from a Marxist perspective.

53 ——, "Literary production and reception," *New Literary History*, vol. 8, no. 1, 1976, pp. 107–26. Translation of sections from *Gesellschaft–Literatur–Lesen* concerning the Marxist notions of production and reception (consumption) of literature.

54 —— et al., *Gesellschaft–Literatur–Lesen: Literaturrezeption in theoretischer Sicht* (Weimar and Berlin: Aufbau-Verlag, 1973). GDR's criticism of western modes of reception theory coupled with the development of a Marxist model. Important theoretical essays by Naumann and Karlheinz Barck are followed by historical discussions and applications.

55 *Poetik und Hermeneutik: Arbeitsergebnisse einer Forschungsgruppe* (Munich: Fink, 1964 ff.). This is the series title for the proceedings of the biannual colloquia held at Constance; reception theory and matters pertaining to it have played a major role at these conferences. The individual titles and editors of the volumes are as follows:

   I. *Nachahmung und Illusion*, 1964, ed. Hans Robert Jauss.
   II. *Immanente Ästhetik – Ästhetische Reflexion*, 1966, ed. Wolfgang Iser.
   III. *Die nicht mehr schönen Künste*, 1968, ed. Hans Robert Jauss.
   IV. *Terror und Spiel*, 1971, ed. Manfred Fuhrmann.
   V. *Geschichte–Ereignis und Erzählung*, 1973, eds Reinhart Koselleck and Wolf-Dieter Stempel.

VI. *Positionen der Negativität*, 1975, ed. Harald Weinrich.
VII. *Das Komische*, 1976, eds Wolfgang Preisendanz and Rainer Warning.
VIII. *Identität*, 1979, eds Odo Marquard and Karlheinz Stierle.
IX. *Text und Applikation*, 1981, eds Manfred Fuhrmann, Hans Robert Jauss, and Wolfhart Pannenberg.

56 REESE, WALTER, *Literarische Rezeption* (Stuttgart: Metzler, 1980). A short introduction to the major directions in reception theory. Partially annotated bibliography follows each section.

57 SCHLENSTEDT, DIETER, *Wirkungsästhetische Analysen: Poetologie und Prosa in der neueren DDR-Literatur* (Berlin: Akademie-Verlag, 1979). Endeavor to view recent GDR literature with the techniques of reception theory.

58 ——, *et al.* (eds), *Literarische Widerspiegelung: Geschichtliche und theoretische Dimensionen eines Problems* (Berlin and Weimar: Aufbau, 1981). East German discussion of reflection theory; endeavor to integrate functional model into a reflection framework.

59 SCHMIDT, SIEGFRIED J., *Grundriss der empirischen Literaturwissenschaft* (2 vols) (Braunschweig: Friedrich Vieweg & Sohn, 1980 and 1982). Attempt to write a comprehensive empirical theory of literature.

60 SEGERS, RIEN T., "An interview with Hans Robert Jauss," *New Literary History*, vol. 11, no. 1, 1979, pp. 83–95.

61 SOMMER, DIETRICH, and LÖFFLER, DIETRICH, "Soziologische Probleme der literarischen Wirkungsforschung," *Weimarer Beiträge*, vol. 16, no. 8, 1970, pp. 51–76. Empirical reception study in the GDR; concerns readers' responses to Hermann Kant's *Die Aula* (The School Auditorium).

62 SOMMER, DIETRICH, *et al.* (eds), *Funktion und Wirkung: Soziologische Untersuchungen zur Literatur und Kunst* (Berlin and Weimar: Aufbau-Verlag, 1978). Statistical data used to discuss actual reception and effect; prime example of empirical methods in the GDR.

63 STIERLE, KARLHEINZ, *Text als Handlung: Perspektiven einer systematischen Literaturwissenschaft* (Munich: Fink, 1975). Series of perceptive essays from the early 1970s; endeavor to develop a "systematic literary scholarship" using communication and reception theory, as well as semiotics. See pp. 113–15.

64 ——, "The reading of fictional texts," in Susan R. Suleiman and Inge Crosman (eds), *The Reader in the Text: Essays on Audience and Interpretation* (Princeton: Princeton University Press, 1980), pp. 83–105. Fictional texts as pseudoreferential; see discussion, pp. 111–12.

65 STÜCKRATH, JÖRN, *Historische Rezeptionsforschung: Ein krit-

ischer Versuch zu ihrer Geschichte und Theorie (Stuttgart: Metzler, 1979). Investigates the older tradition of reception studies in the nineteenth and early twentieth centuries, primarily those concerning the impact of one author on the public.

66 TURK, HORST, *Wirkungsästhetik: Theorie und Interpretation der literarischen Wirkung* (Munich: edition text + kritik, 1976). Collection of four essays on different historical aspects of literary effect from Aristotle to the present.

67 VIEHOFF, REINHOLD, "Über einen Versuch, den Erwartungshorizont zeitgenössischer Literaturkritik empirisch zu objektivieren," *Zeitschrift für Literaturwissenschaft und Linguistik*, vol. 6, no. 21, 1976, pp. 96–124. Results of survey sent to West German critics; see p. 136.

68 WALDMANN, GÜNTER, *Kommunikationsästhetik I: Die Ideologie der Erzählform* (Munich: Fink, 1976). Attempt to construct an encompassing communication model. Application to a short story written by a National Socialist. For discussion, see pp. 117–21.

69 WARNING, RAINER (ed.), *Rezeptionsästhetik: Theorie und Praxis* (Munich: Fink, 1975). Excellent reader with a helpful introduction. Includes major essays by Jauss and Iser as well as Ingarden, Vodička, and Gadamer. Some international flavor (Fish, Riffaterre). Divided into theoretical section, replies to criticism, and applications.

70 WEIMANN, ROBERT, *Literaturgeschichte und Mythologie: Methodologische und historische Studien* (Berlin and Weimar: Aufbau, 1974). One of the foremost critics in the GDR and a contributor to the east–west "debate," Weimann is a specialist in English and American literature who here deals with issues of tradition and literary history.

71 ——, "'Reception aesthetics' and the crisis of literary history," trans. Charles Spencer, *Clio*, vol. 5, no. 1, 1975, pp. 3–33. Good summary of the central points of difference between GDR and FRG theorists on the matter of reception.

72 WEINRICH, HARALD, "Für eine Literaturgeschichte des Lesers," *Merkur*, vol. 21, 1967, pp. 1026–38. Important early statement calling for a turn to the reader in writing literary history.

73 WIENOLD, GÖTZ, "Textverarbeitung: Überlegungen zur Kategorienbildung in einer strukturellen Literaturgeschichte," *Zeitschrift für Literaturwissenschaft und Linguistik*, vol. 1, no. 1–2, 1971, pp. 59–89. Discussion of multifaceted operations of reception from linguistic and semiological perspectives.

74 WOLFF, ERWIN, "Der intendierte Leser: Überlegungen und Beispiele zur Einführung eines literaturwissenschaftlichen Be-

griffs," *Poetica*, vol. 4, no. 2, 1971, pp. 141–66. Opts for a reader model based on the author's intended audience.

75 ZIMMERMANN, BERNHARD, *Literaturrezeption im historischen Prozess: Zur Theorie einer Rezeptionsgeschichte der Literatur* (Munich: Beck, 1977). Insightful discussion of reception as a sociological phenomenon. Demand for greater consideration of historical and institutional dimensions.

C **Alternative models**

I have included here only a small sampling of books that approach reading, the reader, or a central concern of reception theory from a different vantage point. For a more complete bibliography of works categorized as "reader-response criticism," see Tompkins (pp. 233–72) and Suleiman/Crosman (pp. 401–24), both cited below.

76 BARTHES, ROLAND, *S/Z*, trans. Richard Miller (New York: Hill & Wang, 1975). Extensive interpretation of Balzac's *Sarrasine* using five "codes." Reading viewed as production of text.

77 BLEICH, DAVID, *Subjective Criticism* (Baltimore and London: Johns Hopkins University Press, 1978). With the demise of scientific objectivism Bleich postulates a new subjective paradigm for all hermeneutical disciplines. Tremendous implications for reading and interpretation.

78 BLOOM, HAROLD, *The Anxiety of Influence: A Theory of Poetry* (Oxford: Oxford University Press, 1973). Reading as misreading; interpretation as misinterpretation. Most concerned with poets influenced by previous poets, it has ramifications for literary theory as well.

79 CULLER, JONATHAN, *Structuralist Poetics: Structuralism, Linguistics, and the Study of Literature* (Ithaca, NY: Cornell University Press, 1975). Introduction to structuralism. Emphasis on competence and conventions as enablers of reading and understanding.

80 DE MAN, PAUL, *Allegories of Reading: Figural Language in Rousseau, Nietzsche, Rilke, and Proust* (New Haven and London: Yale University Press, 1979). Examination of reading from a deconstructive position; endeavor to find aporias between figurative and literal levels of texts.

81 FISH, STANLEY, *Is There a Text in This Class? The Authority of Interpretive Communities* (Cambridge, Mass.: Harvard University Press, 1980). Collection of Fish's theoretical essays from the 1970s. Literary communities and their conventions enable interpretation and account for differences in views.

82 HOLLAND, NORMAN H., *The Dynamics of Literary Response*

(New York: Oxford University Press, 1968). Reader response as a function of the reader's psychology.

83 MAILLOUX, STEVEN, *Interpretive Conventions: The Reader in the Study of American Fiction* (Ithaca, NY: Cornell University Press, 1982). Develops socially based model of reader-response theory. Discussion of Bleich, Culler, Fish, Holland, and Iser. Also sample applications of his theory.

84 SULEIMAN, SUSAN, and CROSMAN, INGE (eds), *The Reader in the Text: Essays on Audience and Interpretation* (Princeton: Princeton University Press, 1980). Essentially a collection of essays on reader-response criticism; includes contributions by Iser and Stierle. Introduction by Suleiman is more related to non-German criticism. Useful annotated bibliography divided into rhetorical, semiotic and structuralist, phenomenological, psychoanalytic and subjective, sociological and historical, hermeneutic, and special volumes.

85 TOMPKINS, JANE P. (ed.), *Reader-Response Criticism: From Formalism to Post-Structuralism* (Baltimore and London: Johns Hopkins University Press, 1980). Excellent reader that gathers major essays by reader-response critics. Reception theory only represented by Iser. Helpful annotated bibliography is especially good for English-language material.

86 WHITE, HAYDEN, *Metahistory: The Historical Imagination in Nineteenth Century Europe* (Baltimore and London: Johns Hopkins University Press, 1973). The necessity of constructing history in accord with various narrative patterns. Has drastic implications for older views of literary history.

D Journals

87 *Amsterdamer Beiträge zur neueren Germanistik* (Amsterdam: Rodopi, 1972–). Vol. 3 (1974) is devoted entirely to reception theory; includes contributions by Gerd Labroisse, Elrud Kunne-Ibsch, Horst Steinmetz, and others. Title of special issue – "Rezeption – Interpretation."

88 *Der Deutschunterricht: Beiträge zu seiner Praxis und wissenschaftlichen Grundlegung* (Stuttgart: Klett, 1948–). Journal concerned with teaching and pedagogy. Vol. 29, no. 2 (1977) on the aesthetics of reception ("Rezeptionsästhetik"); vol. 33, no. 2 (1981) on reading ("Leseprozesse im Unterricht").

89 *Diacritics: A Review of Contemporary Criticism* (Baltimore: Johns Hopkins University Press, 1971–). Interview with Jauss in vol. 5, no. 1 (1975), pp. 53–61; essays on and interview with Iser in vol. 10, no. 2 (1980). Iser–Fish debate in vol. 11 (1981). Otherwise,

occasional essays or reviews on matters related to reader or reception theory. Known mostly for post-structuralist leanings.

90 *New Literary History: A Journal of Theory and Interpretation* (Baltimore: Johns Hopkins University Press, 1969–). Has been most active English-language journal in presenting and promoting reception theory and related issues. Iser, Jauss, and Weimann are advisory editors.

91 *Œuvres et Critiques: Revue internationale d'étude de la réception critique des œuvres littéraires de langue française* (Paris: Edition Jean-Michel Place, 1976–). Vol. 2, no. 2 (Winter 1977–8) was devoted to reception theory.

92 *Poetica: Zeitschrift für Sprach- und Literaturwissenschaft* (Amsterdam: B. B. Grüner, 1967–). Most important journal for Constance School variety of reception theory. Has printed major essays as well as several *Zwischenbilanzen* ("tentative balance sheets") in vol. 7, no. 3–4 (1975), vol. 8, no. 3–4 (1976), and vol. 9, no. 3–4 (1977).

93 *Poetics: International Review for the Theory of Literature* (Amsterdam: North-Holland, 1975–). Publishes occasional essays on reception theory, usually from empirical, linguistic, or semiotic perspectives. Siegfried J. Schmidt is currently the editor, and Norbert Groeben is on the advisory board.

94 *Poétique: Revue de théorie et d'analyse littéraires* (Paris: Seuil, 1970–). No. 39 (Sept. 1979) was devoted to reception theory ("Théorie de la réception en Allemagne") with contributions by Jauss, Iser, Stierle, Warning, Weinrich, Stempel, and Gumbrecht.

95 *Weimarer Beiträge: Zeitschrift für Literaturwissenschaft, Ästhetik und Kulturtheorie* (Berlin and Weimar: Aufbau-Verlag, 1955–). Most important East German journal for literary and cultural theory; has published several important essays on reception theory, functional history, and related matters since the late 1960s.

96 *Zeitschrift für Literaturwissenschaft und Linguistik (LiLi)* (Göttingen: Vandenhoeck & Ruprecht, 1971–). No. 15 (1974), edited by Peter Uwe Hohendahl, on reception theory. No. 21 (1976), edited by Norbert Groeben, on literature and psychology (empirical methods).

Index